CW00455530

HAVE IT ALL WITHOUT BURNING OUT

DEBORAH BULCOCK

WITH GRATITUDE

My deepest and most sincere thanks to the people who have made this book possible.

The whole team at Authors & Co who have made creating, designing and publishing this book such a pleasurable, easy and professional experience.

To my dedicated proof readers, Sandra and Lynne (my mum).

To my clients who have helped make my dream come true. And a special thanks to those clients who have courageously and willingly told their story for this book.

To all my dear friends and family who have always encouraged and supported me.

To every teacher, mentor, coach and guide who has helped me get to this point.

3

And of course, to my four-legged friend Lexi who has patiently sat by my side whilst I've been writing.

CONTENTS

YOUR RESOURCE CENTRE

As you read through this book you may find that you want to reflect and explore things for yourself. That's why I've created a suite of free downloads to help you.

When you see this symbol at the beginning of a chapter it indicates that worksheets are available for you to download and use.

You will find your resource centre at:
www.deborahbulcock.com/haveitall

A BIT OF BACKGROUND

1

INTRODUCTION

Welcome!

This is a book about having it all, without having to burn out to get there. Sharing what makes it increasingly likely for you to achieve that dream, avoiding any pitfalls and false expectations, and making it real and pragmatic amidst our super busy lives.

It is based on my experience as a senior leader in big business, as a qualified health professional, as a coach to busy and ambitious professionals, a consultant to leaders in business, alongside my personal experience of stress and burnout.

It is intended to be an easy yet thought provoking read, providing you with useful information, insight, inspiration, guidance and practical suggestions.

Grab a cuppa and let's get started.

Why Are You Reading This?

My guess is that you, or someone you care about, is experiencing the ill effects of stress in a way that's compromising quality and enjoyment of life, or that there is a search for a path that allows you to reach your end goal quicker and easier. I hear you.

It is likely that at least some of the following will resonate with you and if that is the case then I believe this book will serve you well:

- You have an ambitious nature, are always on-the-go and pushing it to the max, constantly squeezing in something else.
- You don't like to let anyone down and will go the extra mile to do the very best you can.
- You are feeling increasingly tired all the time, even exhausted, and your normal methods for getting your zest back are no longer working.
- Whilst overly tired, you still struggle to relax and sleep well.
- You are finding yourself feeling overwhelmed at things that didn't use to faze you and not really understanding why that is the case – problems may seem insurmountable.
- Your concentration, focus and problem solving

abilities have taken a nose dive, alongside your memory which has run off and left the building.

- You are becoming more highly strung, agitated and frustrated at things that wouldn't normally bother you and it's getting harder to contain that.
- You sense being out of control, just going through the motions, know you are reaching your limit and feel like you need a really long break from everything.
- You have a sense of apathy and lack of motivation that is out of character for you.
- You are feeling trapped, isolated and misunderstood by the people around you whom you can't get to appreciate what is going on for you.
- You want to get out and about outside of work, but you have little energy for doing the social and personal things you used to.
- You may be experiencing health conditions you never had before and can't explain the onset.

Saying yes to these things is not a diagnosis of anything, it is simply a way for you to check in with yourself and review any changes that you've noticed. If there are a number of statements that resonate it could be that you're experiencing the effects of stress.

As I responsibly say to any of my clients, consulting a medical professional is always the first course of action if you have concerns about your health. Use this book as a complement to support your journey to wellbeing and having it all.

Let's Talk Burnout

In 2019 the World Health Organisation (WHO) added burnout to the 11th classification of the international classification of diseases. They described it as an 'occupational syndrome' and emphasised that it wasn't a medical condition.

The WHO definition is as follows:

> "Burn-out is a syndrome conceptualized as resulting from chronic workplace stress that has not been successfully managed. It is characterized by three dimensions:
>
> (a) feelings of energy depletion or exhaustion;
>
> (b) increased mental distance from one's job, or feelings of negativism or cynicism related to one's job;
>
> (c) and reduced professional efficacy.
>
> Burn-out refers specifically to phenomena in the occupational context and should not be applied to describe experiences in other areas of life."

WORLD HEALTH ORGANIZATION 2019

Now I will admit I was absolutely delighted that burnout was being recognised, that people were talking about it, that the spotlight was being shone brightly. For something to be added to the WHO classification of diseases is a big deal and indicates an increased incidence of the condition. I even felt a little validation and a sense of "I told you so!"

Yet, as someone who has been there and got the burnout t-shirt, I believe the definition falls way short. I don't accept that an ill-health condition with those characteristics can be so one-dimensional. We are whole beings; we are affected by all aspects of life. It therefore can't just be a workplace phenomenon. Undoubtedly work played a huge part for me, but it wasn't the only thing, and that plays true for the many colleagues, friends and clients who have been kind enough to share their story with me.

As with many illnesses, how they show themselves across individuals can be slightly different. When it comes to chronic stress and burnout the complaints and phrases I tend to hear the most include:

- Exhausted all of the time.
- Running on empty.
- Overwhelmed.
- Can't think straight.
- Unable to function properly.
- Can't carry on like this.

There are a whole load of other physical and emotional symptoms that can accompany burnout but these phrases are the ones I hear the most and are commonly at the top of any list that you will read.

We don't yet have access to a wealth of data on the incidence of burnout, mainly because it's a newly classified condition and is recognised as a workplace syndrome rather than a specific disease. However, we do know with certainty from a whole range of studies, that the number of people experiencing stress and stress-related ill-health is on the rise, as is the cost to business through sickness absence, reduced productivity and effectiveness.

We don't have the information to confirm whether burnout has reached epidemic status, but what I will say with conviction is that it is a very real and increasing problem. It is not well understood, often hidden and unspoken, and the costs are high – to quality of life, to relationships, to families, to business and society.

What's The Answer?

Whether you believe burnout to be just about the workplace or a whole-person condition doesn't necessarily matter. My objective is to share with you the relevant highlights of my personal experience, professional experience, training and insights with the hope of enabling you to stop burnout in its tracks, have a quicker recovery, or even stop you getting on that path in the first place.

In our modern society where we crave convenience and rely on quick fixes for anything and everything, the harsh reality that the best solutions for avoiding burnout take some inner work and lifestyle change can be an unwelcome message. I get it, we're busy, on-the-go, and haven't got time for all that 'fluffy' stuff!

Well, keep an open mind. Because I was that person; in fact, I still am that person in some respects, as are my clients. My promise is that when you have a deeper understanding of stress, knowledge of how to proactively build resilience and manage your stress response, without it all taking loads of time, you will find a way forward that is right for you.

It only has to start with one small change.

Before we get into the real detail, let me tell you a bit about my story with burnout.

2

BURNOUT AND ME

February 2012

I'm sat at the bottom of the stairs, elbows on my knees and head in my hands, tears flowing. I've just come through the door from work and my tank is well and truly empty. I'm exhausted and emotionally spent, more than I've ever known. I hurt everywhere; it even feels like my bones are aching. My mind is numb, no longer flowing with all the questions that I've been asking myself for some time. *What's wrong with me? Am I seriously ill? Why does everything hurt so much? Why can't I just pull it together? Why can't my doctor find anything wrong? Why is this happening to me?*

I'm done. I can't carry on. I don't even know how to take the next step – literally – I can't get up the stairs.

Looking Back At Burnout

That was seven years ago, from the point of writing this book, and I guess it was my rock bottom.

A seemingly fit, healthy and successful woman completely broken as she approached her 39th birthday. Unable to physically get up the stairs, existing and surviving, rather than living and thriving.

It was hard to describe how I felt at the time, and so I hadn't really told anyone, because I just didn't know what to say. When I tried to do so, people jumped in with advice and comments I found frustrating – *you just need a holiday, you need to quit your job, you need not to care as much, you need to stop taking on so much, just take some time off, it's because of the food you eat, just relax.....* All well-meaning from a place of love, probably all accurate, but completely unhelpful in moments of desperation. It left me feeling misunderstood and isolated.

I know I'm not alone in my experience of burnout. Over the years I've seen others go through their own version, I've read countless stories, I've worked with clients who are approaching it, going through it, coming out the other side, and having recovered.

Telling My Story

I've thought a lot about what led to me reaching that debilitating point of ill-health, and what enabled me to recover. I feel a sense of duty to share the insights and lessons I've drawn along the way, and to provide with you with all the advice I can offer. The learnings are what fuels the passion for my work today, and I hope for a long time to come.

Just remember that we're all different and this chapter is about my particular experience. I'm not implying in any way that this is the only way to experience chronic stress and burnout. Nevertheless, if any of this resonates or triggers a reaction, know you are not alone, it is real, and there is a way forward.

So here's the story of my road to burnout as best as I can explain.

High Achiever

Yes, I'm one of those. For as long as I can remember I've had a strong desire to achieve. From spelling tests in primary school to delivering results in big business, I've always thrown myself into it and done my absolute utmost to get the best results I can.

I didn't believe in just "good enough", it needed to be excellent. Anything less was a failure in my eyes, and failure was not an option. And therein lay one of the problems. We're all human, we all have to learn and grow, and make mistakes, and unfortunately we can't be good at everything.

For many people, making mistakes and the growth process that goes with it is all an accepted and often exciting part of the process. However, for me anything less than excellent served to chip away at my self-confidence and fed the seeds of doubt which grew and grew over time.

You see, being a high achiever doesn't necessarily mean that you achieve everything you turn your hand to, it simply means that you *want, desire and need* to be a high achiever to have any self-worth.

So as I went through life and wasn't a straight 'A' student, didn't get a first class in my degree, didn't get on to the first graduate placement I applied for, wasn't always the top performer at work, had failed relationships, didn't get married, didn't have the life-changing miracle of children, didn't have the physical appearance I strived for … my self-confidence plummeted and doubt pervaded my every waking moment.

Not that you would have known. It was my biggest secret.

People Pleasing Perfectionist

Oh yes, I'm one of those too. With cherries on top! Not only did I want to achieve to the highest level, but I wanted people to be pleased with me for doing so. I never needed public accolades, in fact that would mortify me, but I craved praise, recognition and thanks.

So when I was pleased with something and others weren't, then my sense of achievement was lost. External validation was really key for me. And if I'm honest it still is a little – even as I've been writing this book I've been wondering who I can send it to for feedback, clearly pre-selecting those people who will be kind to me.

Having this trait as part of your make-up can make it really difficult to say no, even to express a different opinion in a discussion. So you find yourself frequently conflicted, keeping comments and opinions 'unsaid', doing things you don't really want to do, stretched to the max because you've over-committed, over-doing tasks because you need them to be perfect, and over-thinking everything that's happened. Oh, the over-thinking, it's exhausting.

You wouldn't know though. It's not something I speak about because I'm a high achiever.

Hating Conflict

I've touched on this, but let me emphasise the extent of it. I hate *any* form of conflict. Disagreements, arguments, passionate debates, spats and squabbles. It can be friendly and healthy and still have the same impact. And I don't just mean with me involved, it can simply be me observing, passing by or watching on TV.

I'm talking debates over dinner with friends, a couple having a lovers' tiff, disagreeing with someone's point of view, having to complain about poor service, watching anything on politics (although let's face it, there's more than a bit of conflict to get frustrated about there!). All of it makes me want to close my eyes, put my fingers in my ears and shout "LA-LA-LA-LA-LA-LA".

Now, many people who know me will be surprised by this as I'm not one to shy away from an issue, I'll say what needs to be said, I'll lead the charge when something needs addressing. So I hate conflict, but I will address it, and ironically there's the conflict.

You wouldn't know though. I'm a high achieving people-pleasing perfectionist and have therefore become competent at outwardly managing these situations. Not so much inwardly, although certainly better than I used to be.

Deeply Held Values

It's very reasonable to ask why I would do that. If I hate conflict as much as I say, why have I run headlong into those situations with great frequency?

The only way I can explain it is that I *feel* my values very strongly. That's right – I don't just know what they are, but I feel them at the very core of my being. Yes, I know that's what a value should be, but I'm always surprised at how strongly the physical and emotional bonds are to them.

My core values are loyalty, fairness, honesty and integrity. They drive the way I behave and the way I expect others to behave too. They steer how I navigate life, the decisions I make, my behaviours and interactions, how I view and interact with the world, what I enjoy and what I dislike, how my relationships are formed, how I choose whom to trust and so on.

So when these values are compromised, my reaction is overwhelming. My stomach churns, my chest, throat and shoulders tighten, my jaw clenches, it occupies my mind and distracts me, it can prevent me from sleeping and eating well, and it ultimately has the power to ruin days and weeks.

You wouldn't know though. I'm a high achieving people-pleasing perfectionist who hates conflict – I keep those reactions locked tightly away.

Pushing On Through

I'm a grafter, I work hard, I pride myself on it. When something is done, I'll look for the next thing. If there's a problem to solve it gets tackled. If there's a deadline to meet, it will be met. If someone needs help, I'm there. If I've over-committed, that's my problem and I'll sort it.

And how did I do that? By pushing on through. Feeling the fear/exhaustion/stress/conflict…. and doing it anyway. I've worked more early mornings, late nights, weekends and national holidays than I care to remember. But at least the job got done.

Don't get me wrong, I thrived on this for many years. It's what I knew and it's what had led to my success academically and in business. I was the person who would always get things done, no matter what. Through my late-teens and 20s I'd go as far to say that it was the fuel that drove me and I actively sought out the additional pressure. Into my 30s though it became a different matter.

You wouldn't know though. I'm a high achieving people-pleasing perfectionist who hates conflict and values loyalty – and let's face it, I'll just push on through.

Wanting To Know Why

For many people the natural reaction to all of this is to ask why. Why are you a people-pleaser? Why are you a perfectionist? And whilst the people-pleaser in me fears your disappointment, I have to tell you that's not the purpose of this book, nor how I can best help you. And I don't claim to be a counsellor, psychotherapist, psychologist, neuro-linguistic programming practitioner, or anyone else formally qualified in the workings of the mind.

Nevertheless I am highly self-aware and insightful with a massive dollop of emotional intelligence thrown in. I've sat in the therapist's chair and I've done the work.

What's important right now, to allow me to help you, is to appreciate the consequences of all of this and how it relates to burnout.

So What?

You now know I'm a high achieving, people-pleasing perfectionist who hates conflict, feels her values deeply and always pushes on through. Nice to meet you. Why is this important and relevant to this book?

The reason I have chosen to bare my soul is not for the purpose of self-indulgence, although I will admit the process is extremely therapeutic. No, the reason is to illustrate to you how our individual make-up combined with our experiences and environment can create the perfect recipe for chronic stress and burnout if we don't recognise what is going on and have strategies to handle it.

A Bit Of Background

Let me first give you the "in a nutshell version" of my work history. I've had a fairly standard yet privileged education and career path – school, college, university, then the world of work in big corporates within the Financial Services sector. I excelled at work through my 20s with consistent glowing appraisals, promotions in quick succession and comments of "you'll go far". At the age of 27 I think I was the youngest person to reach the management grade I was at in the history of that company at the time. It raised a few eyebrows.

Having moved "back up north" in my late 20s, my opportunities in that company became more limited and I started to move around to different companies, enjoying similar levels of success. I chopped and changed between contracting and permanent roles to suit my needs at the time. I was earning good money, was highly regarded, worked with some wonderful people and met some of my dearest friends.

Fast forward to 2012 when the bottom fell out of my world and I found myself sat on the bottom step unable and unwilling to move. I knew I had to do something drastically different to allow me to recover. I took a bit of time off, I went back to work contracting part-time 3-4 days per week, enrolled to study Nutritional Therapy for three years and my new path was born.

The path has been pretty winding since then with lots of twists and turns as I've tried new things, discarded some, kept some, and kept going until I've reached a point of feeling "this is it; this is what I want".

There's so much more I could tell you, but I really want to get back to the point of the story. And that is to highlight the ingredients of the perfect recipe for my burnout experience.

Perfect Recipe For Burnout

I've told you the traits that I believe contributed to my burnout, and you've had a peek into my work and life history. Whilst I want to emphasise that the majority of my work experiences have been enormously positive and rewarding, it has been a key part of my recovery for me to understand and pinpoint the factors involved in my ill-health, and that included work.

Here are some examples of how my environment, experiences and personality collided, ultimately manifesting as stress, then chronic stress, then burnout:

- A fast-paced, high performance work environment that rewarded significant effort and results – fuelling my desire to push on through and igniting my high achieving, people-pleasing tendencies.
- Frequent exposure to behaviours in work, and occasionally outside, that seriously compromised my values set and catapulted me into a state of conflict.
- Delivering business objectives that I didn't always agree with, didn't feel were right for our people or customers – trying to steer a different course and therefore often finding myself in conflict with others.
- Operating at a senior level in big business naturally came with disagreement, tough decisions and

keeping secrets – all a typical day at the office, but pressing buttons for me nonetheless. Not always being able to be honest and straight with my team because something was confidential wasn't an easy task for me.

- Experiencing first-hand some bullying behaviour, and choosing to stand up to it, despite the lack of peer and HR support for my situation – my values challenged all over the place. This was a particularly difficult couple of years.
- And personally, a whole load of life stuff that took its toll – relationship breakdown, moving location, changing job and companies, the realisation I wouldn't have children, and a couple of health scares thrown in.
- The list goes on, but you get the idea.

I understand that many people could write a similar list. Maybe you are even nodding in recognition as you are reading. These are things that people deal with day-in and day-out. You may even think there's nothing overly traumatic in there. Looking at things in isolation I'd totally agree, and I believe that's the tricky part about something like burnout and many aspects of mental ill-health. It's not just one thing at one point in time, although most people you do have the courage to speak to about it would prefer to attribute it to one variable. It's human nature that we want to understand and this can be hard to get your head around.

But when you put the whole lot in one big pot, secure the lid and let it simmer for several years, the outcome was never going to be a positive one.

My Lessons

I've not only had the benefit of hindsight and the opportunity to reflect and explore, but I'm also driven by a desire to stop this happening again – to me and to anyone else.

The main lessons I've been able to draw from my experiences include:

- Burnout doesn't tend to happen overnight: rather, it's a long build up. You might feel that one thing has pushed you over the edge, but it will have taken some time to get to the edge in the first place. I believe my journey to burnout was at least ten years, likely longer.
- Chronic stress will show up in many ways and your body will give you plenty of warning signals along the way. Physical and emotional symptoms are something to tap into and understand, not ignore and silence. My body provided me with untold warnings that things were wrong, but of course I pushed on through until I couldn't continue.
- It's amazing how much abuse the body can take, and how forgiving it can be when you change course, allowing recovery to be possible.

Nonetheless, when we push ourselves to the limit for long periods of time there is the possibility of long term damage. Making peace with that is really important, secure in the knowledge that our battle scars make us stronger.

- And most importantly, it is possible to have it all. You've just got to know what your "all" is!

Advice To My Younger Self

I can't say with certainty that I would have listened; in fact, I'm sure some wise people in my life will have said these things to me at some point in time. What I would say with the benefit of hindsight is simple and straightforward, and if it means something to you, please go with it.

- Know what brings you joy and grab it in abundance – don't allow being a responsible grown-up to prevent this.
- Carve out your own path, avoiding the "musts" and "shoulds" – focus on what you really want.
- Seek advice from the people you truly admire, and then select those nuggets that feel right for you – just because someone offers advice doesn't mean you have to take it.
- Trust your intuition – thinking and analysing every single thing is over-rated.
- Keep it simple and light-hearted – avoid the complicated, it just gets messy.

Today's Truth Bomb

Many of the personal stories told in these kinds of books finish with the perfect happy ending – an aspirational image of a stress-free life, and a beautiful family, in a stunning home, flooded with riches, travelling the world enjoying a laptop lifestyle, living off salad and green smoothies.

I hate to burst your bubble, but I'm just a normal woman from the north of England, riding the rollercoaster of life with flaws and challenges, living anything but the Instagram-worthy perfect life. Chaos and despair can hit me just like anyone.

And just because I've experienced burnout, learned all my lessons, and know everything that I do, doesn't make me immune to reverting to type and making a few bad calls. I would argue that no-one has it completely nailed!

But let me tell you this:

- I experience joy every single day.
- I appreciate the small freely available things more than I could have ever imagined.
- I'm more in alignment with my values than I've ever been.
- I know who I am, who I'm not and I'm (mostly) not afraid to show it.
- I no longer crave the status and success symbols

that drove me in the past, releasing me from the 'need' to earn a lot through a high salary.

- I choose how I spend my days, what I do, who I spend my time with, and it creates an enormous sense of freedom.
- I LOVE what I'm doing for a living.
- And I *believe* I deserve to have it all.

Why Write This Book?

I'm passionate about helping people thrive and succeed. I'm determined to reduce the incidence of burnout. I know from feedback that when I'm working with people 1-2-1 or in my workshops I have the ability to make a difference – and I mean a real difference – to someone's life. And that is the ultimate satisfaction for me.

Having loved coaching people all of my working life and more recently turned coaching into my full-time profession, I've learned what information, insights and advice typically help people move forward with their own purpose, passion and joy. That's what I want to share in the hope of making a difference for you, your loved ones, your colleagues.

If you can take just one insight that makes a positive difference in your life, then I'm smiling.

UNDERSTANDING STRESS AND RESILIENCE

3

STRESS

Let's Talk Stress

A sense of overwhelm or being unable to cope due to pressures which we can't manage.

One of the most enlightening and fascinating moments for me when I was training to qualify as a Nutritional Therapist was really understanding the subject of stress from a physiological perspective as well as the emotional. Given my experiences and personal interests I already believed I understood a lot about stress. I saw it as a negative part of the human make-up, I knew it affected all of us in a multitude of ways, I'd heard about the "stress hormone" cortisol, I knew it was hugely present in my life and those of many colleagues and friends, and I believed I'd found some of the answers to keeping stress at bay.

My training took me on a much deeper journey of learning, and the whole subject piqued my interest so much I knew instantly it would become my area of specialism moving forward. It not only taught me the physiological aspects of stress, but also how to think of the stress in my own life quite differently. My objective in this chapter is to share with you the most powerful insights that had an impact for me, and which continue to do so with my 1-2-1 clients, programme delegates and attendees of workshops on this subject.

Whether this is new information or a recap on some things you already know, I encourage you to read it with fresh eyes, an open mind, and with the capacity to reflect. I'll be asking you some questions along the way to help you tap into what's relevant to you specifically. It's a real opportunity to begin considering what works well for you and what you may want to adjust.

The Purpose Of The Stress Response

Stress is a basic and essential physiological response, and whilst it is complex in nature it is quite simple in its purpose. With stress so often being thought of as a negative we often overlook the true purpose of it which is both positive and essential. We have a primal instinct to survive and the stress response supports that by helping us stay safe from harm, protecting us from danger, allowing us to adapt to circumstance quickly, and motivating us to make decisions and take action in the moment.

One of the fascinating things about the stress response is that it is triggered with any perception of danger; *perception* being the key word. At one point in our evolution our stress response would have helped to protect us from life-threatening situations such as the danger of being attacked by a predatory animal or rival tribe. In today's world the variety and frequency of *perceived* threatening situations is significantly greater, and so the stress response is triggered into action more and more.

It can be helpful to consider a time when you know without any doubt that you've experienced an acute stress response. By acute I mean sudden and extreme. It is usually something that has been unexpected, happened quickly, and you are on the spot to respond. For example, I remember with absolute clarity the moments leading up to a car accident on the motorway when someone crashed into the rear of my car.

It was dusk, rush hour and all lanes of the motorway were very busy. The cascade of brake lights started ahead and I followed suit decreasing my speed, immediately also taking a look in the rear-view mirror. The car behind me was not slowing down at all. As I think about it now, I still know my "normal response" would be to brace for impact. However, my stress response was to accelerate through the distance between myself and the car in front whilst sounding the horn of my car. The driver's response to the sound of the horn was instant, slowing immediately. The car still hit me, but I know the speed and severity of that collision was reduced due to those actions. I can't even remember thinking about it.

I was understandably shaken afterwards, but in the instant that I had to take action I was calm and focused. The decision to speed up was like second nature. And that's the kind of phrase that people tend to use about those situations. *I didn't have time to think. It just came naturally. It was instinct. I don't know how I did that.*

Those types of situations are exactly what the stress response is designed for – helping you to survive and stay safe in situations of potential harm.

Can you recall situations like this? Can you remember what happened for you and what it felt like at the time and then afterwards? It can be helpful to create insights from your own experiences to bring it to life.

When Stress Is Positive

Understanding the purpose of the stress response helps us to appreciate that fundamentally it is positive. Additionally, a certain level of stress can have a positive impact on our day-to-day performance. Have you ever found yourself absolutely in the zone, super productive, getting things done, resolving problems and feeling unstoppable? You're energised, focused and motivated and feel you are performing at your best.

Well there's a term for that and it's called 'eustress'. It relates to beneficial stress where the optimal amount of stress allows us to perform at our peak. This is an empowering way to think about stress; it helps clarify that our goal shouldn't be to eliminate stress completely, but find what helps us reach eustress as much as possible and experience distress as little as possible.

Diagram 1 is a simplified, but impactful representation of this. When we don't have enough stimulation or stress we can actually experience distress because we are fed-up, bored and experiencing a level of apathy. At the other end of the extreme is when stress levels have become too high, we suffer the health consequences, and subsequently our performance reduces. But the sweet spot in the middle of all this is where the magic can happen – eustress becomes the goal.

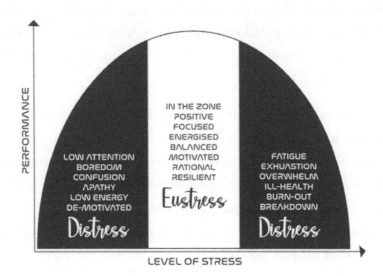

In the zone
POSITIVE
FOCUSED
ENERGISED
BALANCED
MOTIVATED
RATIONAL
RESILIENT

LOW ATTENTION
BOREDOM
CONFUSION
APATHY
LOW ENERGY
DE-MOTIVATED

FATIGUE
EXHUASTION
OVERWHELM
ILL-HEALTH
BURN-OUT
BREAKDOWN

Diagram 1

"How do I find my eustress?" I hear you ask. In short, much of this is about self-awareness and knowing what works for you. We'll go into more detail about achieving eustress and building resilience in later chapters, but right now consider the following basics:

- Think of a time when you believe you've been operating at your very best.
- What were you doing?
- Who were you with?
- What environment were you in?
- What can you remember thinking and feeling during and afterwards?

- Has this happened more than once? What were the common factors?
- Which factors can you replicate in other parts of your life?

Try a couple of different scenarios to explore this further. For example, I know what I need to be at my best when I'm creating and that's very different to what I need when I'm required to problem solve. It doesn't matter if you don't know the answer right now, simply take the time to reflect and be curious with yourself when you have one of those moments. Because you will have moments in which you naturally perform more than others.

Just to manage expectations ... we can't expect ourselves to be in eustress 100% of the time! Life is the proverbial roller-coaster and we need to move up and down the stress scale to learn what enables us to thrive, grow and develop. Nevertheless, I do believe that we can all proactively create more eustress in our lives and reap the benefits from doing so.

How The Body Responds

When we experience stress it's a whole-body response, although there are two fundamental systems which imme-diately kick into action – our nervous and endocrine systems. They initiate a set of protective reactions and responses involving hormones and neurotransmitters to help us stay safe from harm. These reactions result in a whole host of physiological changes.

In a stressful situation we need to be alert, able to act fast and have the energy to do so. As a result:

- Blood pressure increases in order to get oxygen and nutrients to the brain and muscles as fast as possible.
- Glucose is released and blood sugar elevates to provide increased amounts of quickly accessible energy.
- The release of the hormones cortisol, adrenaline and noradrenaline all contribute to the state of high alert and help the brain watch out for danger, continually reassess, and make quick decisions. Instinct and reflexes become more dominant, enabling immediate motivation and action.
- Some systems are completely de-prioritised because they are not important in an imminent life-threatening situation. Resources are re-directed from both the digestive process and sex hormones, as both are considered non-essential at this time.
- Because we are at risk of injury, our blood will also thicken to help prevent the risk of bleeding-out should the body suffer a wound.

There's much more than this going on, yet you'll get a sense of it from this list. Understanding this amazingly sophisticated web of interactions is what helped me realise the beauty of stress and how it is there to positively serve us. With a better understanding it also becomes easier to appreciate certain symptoms in ourselves when we are feeling stressed. Some people talk of feeling their pulse rise, or becoming short of breath, or an inability to concentrate on anything else – and all of those things are explained by the stress response.

It also helps to create a deeper understanding of how longer term stress can be so closely linked to ill-health conditions and this is what we'll look at next.

Chronic Stress

So far we've been referring to acute stress, that which is immediate, extreme and a perceived threat to life. It is acute stress that the physiology I've described is perfectly designed for. Unfortunately, what we are facing in today's world is an increase in chronic stress, referring to long-term, largely continuous stress.

In today's society we tend to lead relentlessly busy lives requiring us to be 'on' all the time, multi-task to the max, squeeze one more thing into our already jam-packed schedules, and have more and more to be considered 'successful'. We are no longer switching off, relaxing or sleeping in ways that our body and mind need. This constant fast-paced and high-pressure lifestyle drives us into a state of chronic stress.

Experiencing chronic stress doesn't mean that you're not functioning or achieving; it simply means that you are putting your body and brain under an unsustainable amount of pressure. At some point in time it is probable that something will fail as a consequence.

Just think about some of the mechanisms of the stress response described above, and consider the consequences if those things continue long-term.

- Increased blood pressure and a thickening of the blood could lead to the increased risk of cardiovascular events such as heart disease, stroke or deep vein thrombosis, for example.
- The brain being on constant high alert can make us more prone to anxiety.
- Digestion being constantly de-prioritised can lead to a whole host of digestive symptoms, conditions such as irritable bowel syndrome, nutrient insufficiency as we fail to digest our food well, and even impaired immunity.
- If blood sugar remains high or constantly imbalanced, then the onset of type 2 diabetes could be a risk.
- Sex hormones being low on the priority list can increase the risk of hormone imbalances, lack of libido, sexual function and fertility.

- Similarly, when cortisol remains high, the production of that hormone gets prioritised over all others, and long-term this can lead to a variety of hormone imbalances.

Whilst this might not be the most uplifting part of this book, it is one of the most important messages to hear. *Really* hear. Our bodies are not designed to be in a constant stress state – the function is for short-term situations. You may not be noticing anything right now, but be under no illusion that chronic stress has consequences if you are not taking consistent, positive action to manage it. Most commonly people tend to talk about persistent tiredness, not being able to cope with the number of things they used to, experiencing a sense of overwhelm where they didn't previously, not being able to think clearly, dealing with poor memory and concentration, increased agitation or frustration, and as a result an overall reduction in their day-to-day enjoyment of life.

Some of the things I've heard most commonly from clients:

- I'm on my knees, but just need to make it through to the next holiday.
- I plan a holiday every three months because I can't survive for any longer without one.
- I wake up feeling like I've got a hangover, then remember that I'm so tired this is how I wake up feeling every day.

- I get shingles probably once a year when I'm run down – I've got used to it now, usually around December/January.
- I used to be really vibrant in the morning, now I'm struggling to peel myself off the mattress.
- The day is like wading through treacle with only half a brain in gear; everything takes so much more effort.
- And much more – digestive complaints, headaches and migraines, skin issues, increasingly anxious, confidence taken a beating, and so on.

Chronic stress will pop up somewhere, sometimes in the most unexpected places. It can be different for everyone, so don't ignore any unexplained physical or emotional symptoms or changes – they are your body's early warning signs encouraging you to listen up and take action. Chronic stress can also exacerbate the symptoms of long-term illnesses or slow-down the speed at which you recover from any illness.

I know this may come across a bit "preachy", but having been there and got the t-shirt I can tell you the end outcome is not pretty or easy to deal with. I was all of those things described above and much more. My warning signs included poor sleep, low energy, variations in mood and confidence, a menstrual cycle all over the place, fluctuating and stubborn weight, constipation, brain fog and frequent muscle injuries to name but a few. My response – push on through (to my next holiday). And I did, until I was sat at the bottom of those stairs!

Managing Stress Matters

Being able to proactively and consistently manage stress is clearly critical to our wellbeing, sense of fulfilment, performance and relationships with others. Each and every one of us has something to gain from reducing stress, managing stress, and investing energy in building resilience. I also firmly believe that there are much broader and far-reaching benefits for society too.

With a reduced incidence of chronic stress and burnout I believe that:

- The burden on our health and emergency services would be reduced.
- Businesses would enjoy enhanced attendance, productivity and innovation.
- Families and communities would live an increasingly harmonious existence.
- Accidents and mistakes in all and any walks of life would be reduced.
- We would be healthier physically and emotionally.

I know this can sound like a far-fetched utopia, yet when we understand more about how stress contributes to ill-health, disputes, crime, accidents and mistakes then it's not as crazy as it may first seem.

I do a lot of work with businesses to help improve the understanding and impact of stress in the workplace, as well as what both employer and employees can each do to make improvements. The size of the prize is enormous for both parties and the knock-on impacts into families, communities and society will be significant too.

According to the Health & Safety Executive Stress Report (2018) 15.4 million working days were lost due to work related stress, depression or anxiety in Great Britain across 12 months in 2017/18. The impact of this lost time cost employers £26 billion or the equivalent of £1,035 per employee, per year. These figures are staggering even though it's likely that any absence due to stress and mental ill-health will be under-reported and therefore larger in reality. Just think if even a third of that could be saved and the difference it would make.

Resilience

I think of resilience as *the ability to adapt well to challenges and bounce back quickly,* rather than simply the strength to face adversity or having mental toughness. It is critical that we have the capacity and capability to be able to adapt at the time, but also be able to subsequently bounce back.

We often consider people to be resilient when we observe them successfully spinning lots of plates, solving problems, striving forward with their plans, and appearing unaffected by the pressures they clearly face on a daily basis. Or it might be one extremely stressful scenario that you've seen them handle well and move on from without breaking stride. We see this adaptation and competent handling of a situation and understandably assume resilience.

What we don't often have is the privilege of seeing how well that person is bouncing back. What are they like behind closed doors? Are they still as energised and motivated in other parts of their life? How is their health? Are they enjoying things as much as they used to? I can't emphasise enough how important this aspect of resilience is.

I was always considered resilient in work and life, able to take on some tough roles and make a difference whilst faced with many challenges. I was certainly able to adapt to new situations and always had both the conviction and courage to tackle issues, work hard to do the right thing, and care for people on the journey. With the benefit of hindsight, I know I wasn't resilient. Yes, I was courageous, I could cope at the time and give a mighty strong performance, but my ability to bounce back was poor, and that meant that over time I became unwell and increasingly ineffective.

My advice is just because someone appears resilient in dealing and coping with stressful situations at the time, always be genuinely supportive and interested about how they are bouncing back.

Many of us are intrigued where resilience comes from, especially when some people appear to be more naturally resilient than others. The explanations that are commonly discussed include:

- Resilience comes with age and experience – the more we experience and understand the likely outcomes of situations and actions, the less those things cause stress, and the more resilient we become.
- Resilience arises from having experienced tough, and sometimes traumatic, situations – once you've been through such a situation, other things just don't affect you the same.
- Resilience is higher for those who don't have much stress in their life – they've got more in the tank to deal with a difficult situation when it comes along.

And of course there's truth in all of these statements – our resilience in coping with the stress in our lives is absolutely influenced by these factors.

My problem with this, however, is that it all appears somewhat passive and reactive. We'll wait to get older, for things to happen to us or for the number of stressors in our life to reduce. Surely if we want to manage and reduce stress for all the reasons we've talked about there has to be something proactive we can be doing. The answer is YES, there are many things we can be doing on a frequent and consistent basis to increase our own levels of resilience.

In a later chapter we'll cover the proactive resilience-building tools that you can call on – there are many you can choose from. First let's reflect on stress, resilience and you.

4

STRESS, RESILIENCE AND YOU

Stressors

A stressor is quite literally something that causes a state of stress or tension for an individual, and the more I explore this subject with clients the more I appreciate the intricacies of individual perception. Ask a group of people what causes them stress and you know you'll get a broad variety of responses. Yes, there will be some common themes, but when you dive into the detail of what specifically is going on for them, there are usually nuances that make each person's experience different.

What's also interesting is that some people are not really sure what causes them stress, and this is more frequent than you may first think. They may say work, but aren't sure what it is about work that they are finding challenging. The more we can have clarity on what is specifically causing us tension and stress, the more likely we are to be able to do something about it. That's what I'd like to focus on right now.

Let's think of stressors in four broad categories, driven by their likely frequency and impact in life.

- Life Event Stress – those things that happen in life that we consider significant: a milestone, a turning point, the start of something new, potentially something traumatic, and taking you out of your comfort zone. The frequency of these events should be low compared to the other categories, but the stress impact will likely be high. There are plenty of positive yet stressful events such as moving house, starting a new job, planning a wedding and getting married, having a baby or starting your own business, for example. Dominating this category, however, tends to be those events with sadness, upset or distress associated. This might be bereavement, redundancy, relationship breakdown, business failure, being the victim of a crime, and so on.
- Situational Stress – those certain situations we find ourselves in that cause us a level of stress. These are unlikely to be everyday occurrences, so not too frequent; however, they can easily generate a state of tension for us. This can cover a whole range of situations – delivering a big presentation, spending

holidays with your extended family, a certain type of social occasion, a particular mode of transport, or even meeting new people. The list is long and varied.

- Daily Routine Stress – you know, those things that happen frequently as part of our daily routine but still manage to cause us some temporary stress. Leaving things until the last minute and then running late, the struggle to get the whole family out of the door on time in a morning (and the fear of picking your children up late), public transport delays, the volume of emails at work, certain meetings that you find pointless, someone being late for your meeting/appointment, and so on. This is the category we can have some real influence over, even if we don't first think so.

- Micro Doses of Stress – a term I first heard used by Dr Chatterjee and which he describes in detail in his own book and podcasts. We're talking here about largely imperceptible stressors, things so slight that we wouldn't consider it a stressor, but by its very nature it will cause a small stress response. This could be stubbing your toe, getting a shock when the water in the shower is unexpectedly cold, something making you jump or giving you a surprise, the blue light from your phone hitting your eyes in the middle of the night when you go to check the time, for example.

It can be really valuable to consider all these types of stressors for yourself so you can objectively appreciate what you are handling right now, along with considering what action you can take to reduce the stress-load.

Take a moment and really consider the stressors in your life. Which are the most frequent? Which have the most impact? Which can you do something about? Which are completely outside your control? Write them down if possible. Getting clear and conscious about this is a great first step. Don't worry if you can't decide how to reduce or manage them immediately – if it was easy you'd have likely already taken action. Just trust that getting really clear on what specifically is causing you stress will undoubtedly help you move forward.

We all have a certain capacity for managing stressors effectively, and I'm sure you know what it feels like when that threshold is being breached. That's why it can be useful to think of your stressors in some detail and use both logic and intuition in determining how to make things not only manageable, but also enjoyable.

If you're dealing with a life event stressor at the moment you'll know that a significant portion of your capacity is already taken in dealing with that, and therefore the opportunity to reduce other stressors in your life will be key to keeping yourself well and avoiding the risk of burnout.

The other thing I would encourage you to do is understand other people's stressors – you may be surprised at what you find. There are two specific groups I'd suggest you have this discussion with as soon as you feel able, the first being your loved ones at home. Now, I clearly don't want to start any domestic arguments and this isn't an excuse to start pointing out the failings of your nearest and dearest! This is about having a good discussion about the things in your life that are causing you stress and seeing how you can help each other to reduce that.

The second is the people you work with most closely at work, or the people who you employ in your business. I often run workshops with work-based teams focused on the subjects of stress and resilience. One of the most powerful conversations can be this one, as long as it's happening in a safe and trusting environment. Understanding your colleagues' stressors, whether at work or home, can help deepen relationships and build a support system that wasn't there previously. Often very simple adjustments can be made to address a stressor, or at least significantly reduces the impact.

A bit of self-reflection and quality discussion can be very powerful.

Signs Of Stress

It's also good practice to understand how stress shows up in you, so you can quickly recognise it, and then respond positively. It is normal for the signs of stress to be different between people and for each of us as individuals to have a range of responses that tell us when we're experiencing stress.

The signs of stress usually show themselves physically, emotionally and behaviourally and it is common for us to experience something from each of these areas. Remember that the purpose of the stress response is one of survival and protection, and we previously looked at the changes that occur. As we understand more about the purpose and physiology, it becomes easier to appreciate how and why stress shows up in the way it does.

Here are some examples.

- Physical signs - such as muscle tension, jaw clenching, digestive upset or pain, headaches and migraines, feeling tired and having disrupted sleep, experiencing palpitations or hearing the pulse in your head, not being able to concentrate or think clearly. These all make sense when you think of it in the context of being ready to fight for survival or run away, and being on high alert ready to jump into action.
- Emotional signs – people report a wide range of emotions they feel during and after a stressful period. These include feeling low, experiencing sadness and being tearful, feeling hyper, jittery, anxious and confused, or commonly getting agitated, frustrated and angry. We may even cycle

through all of these emotions in a short period of time.

- Behavioural signs – as we experience this whole range of physical and emotional responses, the product is usually some form of behaviour change which you and others will notice. You might have a short fuse and become increasingly intolerant and impatient, potentially becoming aggressive; logic can be replaced with irrational thinking, erratic decisions and behaviour; you may become more passive and have a tendency to withdraw. These are all commonly reported behaviour shifts that accompany stress, particularly when it has become more chronic.

Quite often people don't recognise their own stress signs until after the event (sometimes a *long* time afterwards), and this is particularly true when stress has become long-term. Your stress state becomes your new normal and when others make an observation and ask you if you are stressed it can feel a bit irksome! Sound familiar?

This was definitely true for me. What I didn't truly appreciate until I had made some very drastic changes was that my daily living was simply different variations and levels of a 'fight or flight' response. So when I wasn't "feeling" stressed through a whole load of clear physical signs (neck, shoulder and jaw pain, stomach butterflies and quickened breathing) I thought I was relaxing and recharging. But the reality was I was always 'on', had to be doing something that occupied my mind, or going somewhere to try something new.

Some of the very basic things I noticed once I'd truly shifted my state and was experiencing a sustained recovery from burnout were a surprise to me – because many of them had just been my normal for such a long time. You may spot a theme arising...!

- Whilst I still don't enjoy being delayed in a lot of traffic I no longer get seriously agitated and tense, huffing, puffing and complaining. I'm definitely more mindful in the situation, and am able to tune in to something more positive.
- I'm also not a fan of a queue or things being obviously inefficient in a shop or restaurant, or anywhere. I can remember once being in the queue at a checkout where not only was the cashier really slow, but the customer then produced a handful of coupons. I smiled nicely through gritted teeth, but my head nearly exploded with frustration at the minutes ticking by. This just doesn't happen to me now, and if I ever feel my shoulders rising with tension or any involuntary tutting or sighing I can check myself pretty much immediately.
- I'm sure we all find it irritating when someone doesn't deliver on a promise in a timely way – it's frustrating and inconvenient. But seriously,

this used to annoy me to a level out of all proportion. And if I missed a deadline myself, or forgot something important, my self-critic was in some serious overdrive. I find myself significantly more understanding and inquisitive these days, leaving the blame and criticism behind (mostly!).

As you can probably appreciate from these few examples I recognise that the stress I was experiencing meant anything that wasn't 'just so' or taking more time than I'd anticipated was a stressor. Let's face it, when you're living life that way you'll have stressors coming at you left, right and centre. And when people told me "not to sweat the small stuff" it wasn't helpful, it was just another stressor.

I'm sharing all of this because I know without any doubt that I'm not unique. I listen to such stories each week and can fully empathise with what's going on. The stress response is in long-term overdrive and suggesting to someone they get some perspective, only focus on what's important, and not to sweat it, is as useful as telling someone with a broken leg they will feel better if they get out for a long run.

The first step is always acknowledgement and understanding. Let's work to understand the stressors and work out how stress is showing up in them. One of the most powerful things I've found is to identify someone's 'early warning sign'. It takes quite a bit of self-awareness, insight and discipline to do something useful with it, but again awareness is the first step.

Your early warning sign is simply your first sign of stress – the thing that often creeps in without you noticing it and then continues to escalate until it's hard to stop. Once you are clear on your signs of stress then it's time to get clear on your early signals, the purpose being to create an immediate, positive and helpful action upon noticing the signs.

To illustrate, I have identified a couple for myself. The first is physical and involves my shoulders becoming more and more tense so that they eventually start rising up towards my ears. This used to progress into a painful and hard-to-correct muscular issue, but now I feel pretty well trained to notice it. As soon as I notice, I get up and change my environment and activity along with taking some deep breaths and enjoying a few relaxing shoulder rolls. It takes 5-10 minutes and then I'm back – more clear-headed and productive than if I'd just ploughed ahead.

The second is a combination of emotional and behavioural – when something is feeling overwhelming or in the 'too hard' category then my stress response is one of flight. I put it off, avoid it, pick it up and put it down a thousand times. I used to let this carry on until the pressure was really high and I had to face it head on. It was never as difficult as I'd made it out to be through this cycle of unhelpful thinking and behaviour. When I find this happening today I do a few things to replace the cycle of denial and avoidance. I'll usually do some deliberate reflection about what's driving me into that zone. I may chat it through with a trusted friend or colleague. I quite often 'write it out' in order to flush out the problem and break it down into something manageable. This strategy is more time consuming than my first example. However, it is still significantly more effective and time efficient than going round in circles indefinitely.

So I'd encourage you to get a clear understanding of your own early warning signs, acknowledge what you normally do in that situation, and then work through what would be more helpful to you. I know this is easier said than done as we're often working with well ingrained behaviour patterns. Nevertheless, it is totally possible, and so the prize is there for the taking.

Receiving Help From Others

When we know someone else is stressed, we'll also have a default response – leave well clear to let them manage alone, make a big fuss and offer lots of help, take over by attempting to remove some of the stressors, and many more variations. The problem is that we might be exacerbating the situation if we don't know what's helpful to that person.

In my experience the best approach is to choose your moment and simply ask how you might be able to help them, assuring them that it's OK if their response is that they need some time and space to work things through for themselves. Interestingly, it is frequently the case that the response to this question is "I don't know". A completely understandable response because it's difficult to problem solve when you're in a stress state.

Therefore what I frequently encourage people to do, whilst not in a state of stress, is to reflect and work through what has been really helpful (and unhelpful) to them in the past. It's likely to be a predictor of what we need, and don't need, in the future. The more we have this insight about ourselves, the easier it becomes to ask for what we need in challenging times.

The range of requests can be varied, for example:

- Could you give me some time to try and get my head round it and ask me again in the morning?
- Could you give me some time to talk through this problem and help me find a solution?
- Could you just listen without judgement or suggestion so that I can get this off my chest?
- Are you in a position to take this off my hands? Or do you know someone who is?
- I don't know what I need, but could you just stay with me for a while?
- And the list goes on. The more we are in a position to be able to ask for what we need, the more likely we are to reduce or remove our stressors quickly.

If you don't know the answer to this question, then certainly take some time to work out what it is. Your response will be different according to circumstance and the person asking, but having a sense of it can only serve to be helpful to you. Once you have a good sense, talk to those people around you about what you're typically looking for and ask them the same question – it's amazing how much these conversations can boost relationships and deepen connections.

How Resilient Are You?

So far, we've talked about getting a good understanding of your stressors, your signs and early warning signals, along with getting clear on what you can helpfully do for yourself and ask from others in times of stress. As you've worked through that you'll probably already have a sense of how far along you are at managing and reducing your own stress. And that is certainly a key part of resilience.

As a reminder, resilience is defined as 'the ability to adapt well to challenges and bounce back quickly' and those few words explain an awful lot. We're talking about under-standing our stressors and how they affect us to the extent that we can make decisions and take action that will help us navigate that situation without having any long-term nega-tive consequences for ourselves. That's a lot to expect of ourselves in our busy and stressful day-to-day lives, yet we've all already got some experience and capability that helps us.

Have a look at these questions and consider how many you would answer positively to.

1. Do you understand your specific stressors and how they affect you?
2. Do you know how stress typically shows up in you, physically, emotionally and behaviourally?
3. Do you know your early warning signs of stress?
4. Do you know how to best help yourself in times of stress?
5. And do you take those actions consistently?
6. Do you know what help to ask of others in times of stress?
7. And do you ask for that consistently?
8. Are you typically able to adapt to a situation and effectively manage a stressor?
9. Can you quickly recover and move on from a stressful situation/time?
10. Do you know how to proactively build your own resilience levels?

Whilst there's no scientific study behind this set of questions, I can assure you that more "yes" responses will equate to a more resilient you. If you're answering no, don't know, sometimes, or it depends, then you know there's some action you can take.

The other thing I would suggest you do before we proceed into the next chapter is to make a list of all the things you do already that you believe helps you to manage stress, to look after yourself through stressful times and which makes you resilient. There is no right or wrong answer here, nothing too small – just whatever you feel makes a difference to you for the better. You'll likely be surprised at how long the list already is.

Managing Stress And Building Resilience

The ideal we are looking for is becoming highly attuned to our own needs and having both the motivation and ability to effectively manage stress and have the highest level of resilience possible. I tend to see stress and resilience as the opposing weights on a set of scales, where having a good balance of the two is our ultimate aim. We don't want to be in a situation where we have zero stress as that will lead to a sense of apathy and boredom; but with some level of stress we need strategies for keeping that stress in check and ensuring we don't tip the balance.

I'm deliberately over-simplifying, but go with me. If we have numerous stressors in life yet no habits or strategies to help us manage them in a healthy and sustainable way, the stress will begin to weigh us down and take its toll on our wellbeing and ability to perform.

Unfortunately what often happens is that stress increases, time becomes even more scarce, we sacrifice resilience boosting habits in favour of "getting stuff done" or procrastinating and the vicious cycle begins. However the reality is that the more daily pressure we need to manage, the more focus we must dedicate to building resilience. It always seems counter-intuitive at the time, but I believe it needs to become our default setting.

If you have your scales balanced nicely and then an unexpected stressor blindsides you, adjustments need to be made in order to enable you to manage the situation as best you can. Other stressors need to be reduced and/or resilience building strategies need to increase. Without the changes, stress tips the balance and the consequences are often some form of ill-health and maybe a few steps towards burnout.

The good news is that taking positive action is totally within our gift. Some stressors we can't control, but how we respond immediately and over the long term is, even though it might not immediately seem like that. Once we have that greater insight into ourselves and know what is helpful to us, decision making and action becomes easier. Our objective is to try and keep those scales balanced as much as possible.

Before we leave this chapter, have a think about whether you have good insights into your stressors, your signs, your early warning signals, what is helpful to you from your own actions and the support of others, as well as assessing how balanced your scales are right now. If you're not sure, take some time. There's no race here and I can assure you that your insights will be impactful and empowering.

HAVING IT ALL

5

WHAT'S YOUR 'ALL'?

We all want to have it all, don't we? We've been encouraged from an early age that everything is there for the taking, we can have anything we want if we work hard enough for it, that we deserve to have everything we desire, and that we live in a world where this has never been more achievable. There's nothing wrong with any of this thinking and I still believe them to be true, just viewed through a slightly different lens.

Nevertheless, there is a problem buried deep within this 'have it all' concept, and it's the misunderstanding of what your 'all' is. With the extent of marketing, media reporting, social media and today's idea of the 'perfect life' we have become significantly influenced by other's views and experiences of what having it all looks and feels like. In doing so, we are becoming increasingly disconnected from what truly brings us joy and therefore allows us to experience happiness. And by striving for everyone else's version of your perfect life, we push ourselves hard, often too hard, leading to ill-health, burnout, and dissatisfaction.

I'm not intending to deceive you. You absolutely can have it all. You just have to know what _your 'all'_ is first and I find a good starting point is to appreciate what brings you joy.

Focusing On Joy

Over the years I've found that this is often the best starting point to help someone who is feeling overwhelmed, stressed, lost, disillusioned, dissatisfied, conflicted or simply feeling that things aren't quite right even if they can't put their finger on it. It is something I'll explore with a client once we have chatted through what's brought them to me in the first place, and it helps us positively focus on what's great rather than what's bad or wrong.

There is a whole host of ways to seek the answer to the question of what brings you joy which we'll look at shortly, but at the very core of it is the ability to tune in to what makes you feel great. Not always as easy as it sounds, because the value in this exercise is the ability to get really specific about it. You need to _feel_ it or it's unlikely to be true joy, more what you _think_ to be joy or is actually someone else's joy.

The ability to work out what's right for us as unique individuals is absolutely key to having all you desire without chronic stress and burnout. Following other people's dreams, thinking of what we must or should do, and conforming to someone else's or society's version of success, rather than focusing on what's right for us, can act as a significant stressor.

The more we understand what truly brings us joy, the more we can make conscious choices to have more of it in our lives on a daily basis. And the more we find ourselves experiencing moments of joy, the greater our ability to enjoy more happiness, whilst removing with greater ease the things we no longer want in our lives.

Joy And Happiness

For me, there's a slight but important distinction between joy and happiness and personally I experienced a real shift when I started to focus more on the former than the latter. That's because searching for happiness can lead you to believe that any moment when you are not feeling happy, you have failed in your quest to achieve happiness. Whereas joy by its very nature is momentary; we experience moments of joy all the time and therefore they are easier to come by.

Of course, you may argue that it's just semantics at play here, but I do believe that the language we use has an impact. When someone asks you if you are happy, you may have a clear yes or no answer, but the majority of people will hesitate and then say something along the lines of "yes, most of the time". It immediately makes us feel that we are falling short.

Yet ask someone what's brought them joy that day and the significant majority of people can give an answer. It may be small and simple, but that's all it takes for many of us. Joy isn't one of those words used an awful lot and so we can also re-frame the happiness question – "in what moment did you feel happiness today?" It allows us to focus on the positive and can provide a much needed sense of achievement.

When I stopped asking myself if I was happy and instead turned my focus to having moments of joy, combined with an overall sense of contentment, then my view of the world and my place within it started to change for the better. I would therefore encourage you to do the same.

Feeling vs Thinking

We mostly live in a world where facts, data, science, analysis and logic are the most valued skills we can possess. Undoubtedly they are absolutely and universally critical in all aspects of life, yet what I've observed is that they are frequently prioritised at the expense of more 'feeling-based' skills such as intuition, sensing, judgement and using our experience. With the balance tipped this way, ethics, morals and the use of our conscience are also devalued.

Having studied economics as an undergraduate and then having worked in financial services for many years, I feel I've had significant exposure to that kind of thinking preference and imbalance. The best business cases may not stand up when we use our intuition and judgement – it might just not 'feel' like the right thing to do. But wow, that's a tough conversation to have.

When it comes to how you live your life, choosing joy and the path that's going to give you the greatest chance of long-term happiness, prioritising your wellbeing and fulfilment, then I urge you to ensure you both feel and think. Get a good balance of both. If in doubt, my personal advice is to trust your intuition.

I can't recall how many pro and con lists I've made over certain life decisions, or even fairly minor decisions if I'm truthful. It is a great way to help you think things through, be objective and draw out all the facts. However, it does inherently prioritise thinking over feeling, and unless you layer that into the process you could end up making the wrong decision for you. The important part of that sentence being _for you!_

If you're feeling conflicted over a decision or a course of action, it's often because the logic associated is not aligned with how you feel about the situation. All I can say is, it is OK to trust your intuition, and it is also OK if other people don't understand it – they're not the ones living with it. Taking this step is more empowering than I can describe.

Your Moments Of Joy

You may immediately know what brings you joy in your life, you may not have a clue, or things may have changed to the extent you want to re-examine it. My hope is that you are motivated to validate, explore or challenge what joy is for you.

It's very simple on the surface, but know that it can be difficult to really button it down to something specific enough for you to subsequently action. Having someone to help you in the process can be helpful, so it might be useful to buddy-up on your quest for joy and having it all.

The conversation is straightforward. Ask yourself and each other questions along the lines of:

- What do you enjoy?
- What really lights you up?
- When do you feel at your best?
- What makes you smile so much you can't stop?
- When do you get so absorbed in the moment that you lose track of time?
- What makes you feel really energised and excited?
- When do others comment that you look happy?
- When do you most feel you can just be yourself?

You might come up with an activity, situation, experience or person, for example. Once you've got something to work with it's time for more questions. For example:

- What was it about that situation?
- Who was there and what were they doing?
- What environment were you in?
- What was around you at the time?
- What senses were you using the most?
- What part of the experience did you enjoy the most? Why?
- How did you feel? Emotionally? Physically?
- What particularly did you enjoy? Why?

You get the idea: we're simply trying to get to the core of what brings you joy, what makes you feel great, and what you have the potential to replicate more frequently and in a greater variety of situations.

Let me give an example from my own experience to bring this to life a little.

I worked in financial services for over twenty years and like most people at work there are parts you enjoy, parts that aren't your favourite, and other parts that you really don't like. That's normal and there's nothing wrong with it, we obviously just want the things we enjoy to outweigh the rest by some margin.

I've already shared my story and so you'll know that the balance of this equation started to move in the wrong direction and certainly contributed to my burnout. There were lots of things important to me in my work – achieving objectives, exceeding targets where possible, delivering transformation to help advance the business, leading in a way that helped people grow, develop and enjoy their work, to name but a few.

I was responsible and tenacious in my pursuit of achieving these things. I would talk proudly about such achievements and be relentless in overcoming any obstacles or issues. However, ask me what brought me joy and what I felt passionate about at work, and the answer is quite different.

Was I proud of achieving financial and service targets? Absolutely. Did doing so bring me joy? No.

Did I feel positive and successful when delivering a big transformation project? Of course. Did doing so bring me joy? No.

Was I proud when a member of my team advanced and received promotion? Undoubtedly. Did it bring me joy? So much joy!

OK, let's delve into that a bit further.

Why was that? I get a deep level of satisfaction from seeing people happy in their work.

What specifically? I just really enjoy seeing people grow and develop and be rewarded for their efforts.

What is about someone else's growth and development that makes you feel good? As their manager I like to think I've played some part in that by helping them along the way.

How have you helped them? Through my leadership, coaching and mentoring.

What is it about leadership, coaching and mentoring that you enjoy? I love helping someone to discover what they really want to do, what they're amazing at, what they would like to develop, and supporting them in their quest to achieve whatever they set out to do.

How does it feel when that happens? I'm smiling and can't stop, I'm more relaxed, I have a deep sense of fulfilment, I'm energised, any muscle tension seems to disappear, I feel connected and part of something bigger than just me. It just feels amazing!

I could go on, but the point of all this is that when I was really clear in what part of my job brought me joy, I found ways to get more and more of it, both inside and outside of work. I took on projects that would give me more of this, acted as a mentor across the broader business and invested increasing amounts of time in my own team. It didn't mean I wasn't achieving in my role, in fact it meant that because I was experiencing more joy from this part of my work I was more resilient and accepting of those areas of work I didn't enjoy as much.

I knew for a while that the environment I was working in was no longer right for me, but focusing on what brought me joy about the job and ensuring that I had regular doses of that daily kept me positive, engaged and performing. It is ultimately what has guided me to the work I do today, albeit I'm not saying we all have to completely change career path or leave our jobs!

Here's a simpler example. I know with all of my being that I love to walk in the countryside – it grounds me, helps me solves problems, de-stresses me, encourages me to breathe deeply and I love watching my dog play freely. Not long before I started writing this book I found myself on crutches and unable to get out for a walk for at least eight weeks. That could have been a disaster for me – one of the key things that brought me joy on a daily basis was now completely out of reach. Not wanting to sound too dramatic, I could have found myself in a spiral of despair. But no, I know that I gain deep joy from being out in the fresh air, in green space and watching my dog run and play like crazy. So off I go to an accessible field in the country-side with my dog Lexi, and a ball thrower. My moments of joy continue.

So if you say you enjoy time with your children, delve into what specifically you mean by that. What are you doing and where are you all when you feel the most joy? What is it about you or your children at that specific point?

Or you're in your element when you're exercising. What specifically is it about exercise that you enjoy? Pushing yourself? The people you see at the gym? The freedom of running? How you feel once you're done? You love competing?

What If You Don't Know?

First things first, don't worry or judge yourself because it's more common than you'd believe. When we've been living life at a million miles an hour, spinning lots of plates and just keeping going, it can be really easy to lose sight of what it is that we love. If the question of "what brings you joy?" stresses you out, then take a different approach – the last thing we want is to increase stress!

My suggestion is to focus more on remembering when you were doing something you enjoyed. This could range from thinking about a role at work right through to activities you loved as a child. There will be something there; it's just that we need to silence the noise of today for a while to get to it.

The other option is to focus more on the here and now. If you can go about your day more mindfully, consciously noting times when you felt really good, then it becomes an easier exercise at the end of the day to examine what it was about that time that gave you those feelings. It can be as simple as an exchange in the coffee shop, a lunchtime walk, a specific time in a work meeting, getting home to family at the end of the day – any manner of options.

If this is a hard task for you I would recommend writing things down as much as possible. Taking five minutes towards the end of the day is all it takes – grab a piece of paper, and don't censure yourself or try to make it read perfectly. Simply ask yourself when you had moments of joy that day, get as specific as you can and keep asking why, and you will draw out some helpful insights.

You will get there.

Grab The Low-Hanging Fruit

So it's time for you to get your first win under your belt; this is your call to action. Let's assume you've been able to identify what brings you joy and you've got as specific as you can. If you're lucky you'll be exposed to that all day every day, but my guess is that's probably not the case if you've picked up this book.

The first step is simply to do one thing that allows you to grab the low-hanging fruit. The one thing that allows you to experience that sense of joy just once more than you did yesterday. Be sure to make it easy and accessible – something you can do in the next 24 hours. It's important to seize the moment or you'll either forget or talk yourself out of it.

Don't wait for something to happen first, make it dependent on someone else or having to buy something or go somewhere. Keep it simple so that there are no obstacles to you taking action. As a good friend of mine always says – action wins, every time! And for something like this it's definitely true.

Then be really sure to assess how it felt. If you put an extra tick in the moments of joy box, register that as a big win. If it didn't feel as you would expect then note that as a hugely valuable lesson. Keep this cycle going daily – the more you can practise that new habit the better. You will start to feel the benefit.

Small Steps

I'm a big believer in celebrating the small steps forward. Yes, big giant leaps can be advantageous and powerful, but can also be off-putting or overwhelming, especially in times of high stress. So rather than take no action at all, why not take one small step. It will either take you in the right direction and you'll feel the benefit, or you'll learn a lesson from it. There's not really that much to lose.

If you take a small step every day, then before you know it you've taken yourself to great places much faster than you would have done by waiting for the window of time to take a giant leap. I find it can be a more practical approach in amongst very busy and pressured lives. So, take the small step, acknowledge and celebrate it, and then you're on to the next thing.

It's very relevant to the next chapter where we're exploring the many different ways in which you can proactively build resilience. Rather than trying to do everything all at once which carries a higher likelihood of failure, start small, choose what resonates the most, and take action. Each small step will move you forward.

Is 'Having It All' Possible?

I believe it is. If my personal and professional experience has taught me anything it's that having it all is entirely feasible, but there are two essential factors that must be in place.

First, you must know what 'having it all' means to you. And that means being absolutely clear on what brings you joy and focusing on getting more of it. Not what you think should bring you joy, or what you think will facilitate you having joy at some point in the future even though you're miserable now, or what someone else tells you will bring you joy.

If you're not sure, that's OK, as there are lots of practical steps you can do to find out. Just avoid the common trap of busting a gut for years on end striving for what you thought would bring you joy, only to end up disappointed.

Tuning in to what brings us joy is a continuous process, not a one-off exercise, so keep checking and refreshing as you go.

Second, we must set ourselves up for success by living our life in a way that provides us with the motivation, resilience and health to achieve our version of having it all. You wouldn't expect your car to travel hundreds of miles on only a couple of litres of fuel; so don't expect your body and mind to deliver everything you want to achieve without the nourishment it needs to get there.

6

BUILDING RESILIENCE

W hen we talk of resilience we mean having *'the ability to adapt well to challenges and bounce back quickly'* and in this chapter I'm sharing with you my insights on how we can proactively develop resilience for ourselves. Consider it your stress management and burnout prevention insurance policy – the investment you make in building resilience will enable you to handle stress and bounce back quicker than you might do otherwise.

The things I'm going to share all require some conscious choice, consistent action and habit formation, but by making the right decisions for yourself, it shouldn't feel like a chore or be overwhelming. Rather, it should contribute to your moments of joy and bring you a sense of satisfaction in addition to the benefit of being a resilience booster. And hey, guess what? All of the things I'm sharing are also linked to improved health and wellbeing. An even bigger bonus!

I appreciate that in amongst busy and stressful lives we'd prefer to opt for convenience, the quick fix, the short cut, the overnight results – in fact, isn't there a pill I can just take with my morning caffeine? This is a normal response for many and nothing to feel embarrassed about. There's only so many hours in the day, right?

And that's why I'm going to start with focusing on why this is important to you.

What's Most Important To You? Your 'Why'?

I'll be honest, I used to both cringe and groan when well-meaning people asked me this question in the past. My younger, stressed out, million miles an hour self, would find this question an inconvenience. It would have meant I'd have to stop and dig deep instead of pushing ahead at pace. I didn't need that in my life …. that was until I was sat at the bottom of those stairs asking myself a whole load of different questions.

If you're planning on just skipping through this bit, I get it. However, I would encourage you not to. In fact, I'd urge you to give it a chance – it could be the crux of you avoiding burnout, or recovering at a faster pace, and being able to have it all.

It's the simplest of questions, yet difficult to answer in a specific enough way to subsequently provide you with the motivation and momentum you need. It is getting to the core of why you want to achieve the things you've set your heart and mind on. Some people are really clear on this and others a bit more on the fuzzy side. Let me get this clear at the outset – it's OK not to know this stuff. I didn't even start examining this subject in my own life until I was in my mid to late 30s, when things were not heading in the direction I expected despite all my hard work and 'achievements'.

It is simply what's important to you, what you really care about, the thing(s) that bring you the most joy you could ever imagine, the reason why you do the things you do on a daily basis, some of which you may not even like. You should feel these reasons so strongly that you know it will keep you focused, consistent and motivated.

The trick with understanding what's most important to you is to keep asking yourself more questions until you get to something unique and specific for you. Commonly people will say that their driver is their children, family or partner – completely understandable given these people are your loved ones, your nearest and dearest. But I'd argue that reason in itself isn't really enough, it's best to be more detailed so that it can act as your life compass when needed.

Compare the differences in these statements which are real summaries of client conversations I've had:

- My children – I want to earn sufficient income to give them a nice home and the education and opportunity they desire, whilst showing them it's possible to balance a career and home life.
- My children – I want to be with them as much as possible whilst growing up showing them that family is more important than anything else in life and that we can be happy without lots of money and possessions.
- My children – I want to guide them to be as self-sufficient as possible from an early age, knowing what it means to be resourceful and assertive in a confusing world.

Each client has their children as their most important driver, but what they want for them and want it will mean to them as an individual are quite different.

Of course, our drivers will shift at different life stages. When we start out in the working world it might be to have more independence by moving into our own home and getting a job that enables the financial freedom to do that. As we progress, things will shift and what's most important to us will change with it. That's absolutely fine, the key is knowing your reasons for the foreseeable future, ensuring it has meaning for you, and living life in a way that serves it.

When There's A Gap

Many clients of mine find they have a gap between what's most important to them and how they are living their life – they are experiencing this incongruence on a daily basis and it acts as a sizeable stressor. I can identify with this, and I know many of you will too. It's common to fall into a certain way of life without having had any deliberate plan to do so and then finding it difficult to make a change without consequence. So we carry on telling ourselves it will be fine.

I did just the same. I fell into my industry, found that I was good at some things, stayed, progressed, enjoyed some parts and not others, started not liking it as much, felt stuck and unable to leap off the treadmill, got used to my position and earnings, and didn't want to let go of the status and the boost that it gave my ego. I was stressed, unhappy and increasingly unwell, but was paralysed into inaction. What would I be without the title? How would I earn any money? When have I got the time and energy to work this through? What else can I do at this stage? Then the denial … oh, it's not as bad as I think, just keep on going, I've got a holiday soon. My 'gap' turned into a giant chasm and was certainly a major contributor to my burnout experience.

People can experience the gap in many different areas – their work, their relationships with friends or partners, how they spend their leisure time, the role they play in their broader family, their sexual identity – it can literally be anything. When there's a gap between who you really are and who you are appearing to be to others, it will not only act as a stressor, but it will be an obstacle to you having it all.

Realising there's a gap is usually identified through your feelings; that sense of unease, something not just sitting right with you; or the situation you end up replaying after the event trying to work out what wasn't right. We all experience gaps at points in time; the key is to take note and make a conscious choice to accept it or make a change. If it's a one-off situation it might be the right thing to simply understand it and let it go. If it's a daily occurrence, then it will need addressing in some way if we are to stay healthy, vibrant and achieve all we desire.

As in any situation there are always choices and it's the same if you know you have a gap between your 'why' and how you are living your life. Just make those choices consciously and deliberately rather than sticking your head in the sand. Your decision may be to carry on as-is for a whole host of reasons, or you may make some changes, big or small. Whatever your outcome, it's the right one for you at that moment. Make your deliberate choice and move forward.

Building Resilience At The 'All You Can Eat' Buffet

I know I've taken you on a slight detour there, but for good reason. Proactive resilience building strategies take motivation, commitment and consistency if they're going to serve their purpose. They are all a healthy habit of some sort, so the more you know your 'why' and minimise the gap, the more likely you are to experience more joy and have it all.

The great news is that there is an enormous amount of choice when it comes to building resilience. It's a bit like those 'all you can eat' buffets in that the options of what to put on your plate are endless. There will be some things at the buffet which are familiar to you and you know that you enjoy, so you'll have some of that. Then there are things that you've never tried before but are a little intrigued by and so you might try a little bit. There are some things you've never had, but one of your friends really enjoys it, so you'll give it a go. And then there are those things that are definitely not for you and wouldn't go on your plate even if someone paid you!

You'll likely have the same response as I take you through a number of different suggestions for building resilience. The key is to really focus on what resonates for you, what you are drawn to, what you are intrigued by, and what you'll be avoiding. It's that fine balance between going with what you believe will work for you whilst also pushing yourself a little. And just like the buffet, you can go back as many times as you like – you don't have to overwhelm yourself by piling your plate too high first time round.

Nourish For Resilience

My approach to building resilience is focused on getting the body and mind in the best place possible, creating the right factors for experiencing eustress (the positive stress), and making the best choices on how we spend our limited time. There is no one right answer because we're all so different. You have to choose what nourishes you, and I use the word nourish very deliberately as it conjures up that sense of giving yourself what will make you strong, happy, healthy, and supported whilst continuing to grow and develop.

I focus on nourishing the body, mind, connection, environment and time as shown in Diagram 2. These are the categories that come up most often in discussion, they're the ones I see my clients having success with and you'll recognise many of them as critical foundations of our day-to-day wellbeing.

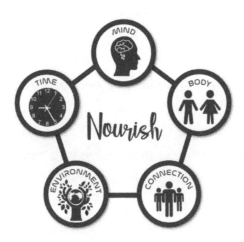

Diagram 2

The next 5 chapters take each of these areas in turn and provide you with a variety of practical suggestions and insights. I encourage you to read them with an open mind, assess what's already working for you, what might be of benefit, and which you are willing to try. Just remember that we're not talking about attempting to do everything at once!

7

NOURISH YOUR BODY

As a Nutritional Therapist I'm sure you'd expect me to start by discussing the power of our bodies and it's the category I'll be going into most detail on. I can't imagine for a second that any of the subjects I'm covering will be new to you, and they certainly aren't rocket science. However, these critical foundations are ones that remain challenging for many, especially when living life at lightning speed and carrying a whole load of pressure.

Given my background you'd be forgiven for thinking I'd start straight away with the subject of nutrition, but no, I'm actually going to start with what I consider the quickest win of all.

Breathe

They say "take a deep breath" for good reason!

Earlier in the book we delved into the stress response to understand the main systems of the body involved and the types of physiological reactions that take place. When we are having a stress response it's the sympathetic part of the nervous system that's activated, more commonly known as the 'fight or flight' response. Conversely, when we're in a relaxed state it's the parasympathetic nervous system in action, also known as 'rest and digest'.

We should spend the majority of our time in rest and digest, with only an acute stressor triggering the fight or flight response, but we know this isn't the case in modern life. We are spending more and more of our time responding to stressors and existing in the fight or flight mode.

When we take some deep breaths or do some meditation we are usually doing it to help us feel calm and more relaxed in that particular moment. The reason this works is that the practice of deep breathing can shift our nervous system from a state of fight or flight and into rest and digest. It's simple, free, accessible anywhere at any time, anyone can do it and it has a profound effect on reducing the stress response. How amazing is that?

The biggest areas of resistance I face when I talk to people about deep breathing include: I don't have the time to just sit and do nothing; I can't ever clear my mind and so it won't work for me; Isn't that a bit 'fluffy'? I'll admit I used to think the same things. But having spent years now understanding the stress response, the benefit is so clear to me, it's a no-brainer. The more we can train ourselves and our nervous system to make the shift into 'rest and digest', the better on every level.

So let's not over-complicate things. There are many breathing techniques you can adopt, and plenty of apps out there that can guide you through a breathing exercise (Calm, Headspace and Insight Timer being my personal favourites). Here's how I suggest you start:

1. Mindful Breathing – the first step involves not changing a thing. It's simply about tuning in to your current breathing rhythm, being mindful of it, observing it and focusing only on the breath. You'll probably find that your breath automatically slows. Try it for 60 seconds and see.

2. Deep Breathing – the most common recommendation I make to my clients is a very simple deep breathing exercise for just 60 seconds, several times a day, every day. Breathe in for a count of 5, hold for 2, and breathe out for a count of 7. If this is too much, try 3-2-5. I suggest associating the breath work with a regular everyday activity – do it every time you boil the kettle or get a drink, or every time you walk to the bathroom, for example.

3. Extended Deep Breathing – if just once in the day

you can extend your deep breathing to three minutes, then five, then ten, you'll start to notice a significant difference. Keep the regular 60-second deep breathing going, but just once in the day extend it. It's all about building up gradually.

4. Meditation – whilst a deep and extended meditation will have more health benefits than 60 seconds of deep breathing I recognise that this can be a step too far for many people. We'll cover it more in the 'nourish your mind' section, but if you're able to take the step to a guided meditation, for example, then you will undoubtedly feel the benefits.

Every step here has benefits. If the step you take is mindful breathing and you manage to do that several times a day that's a fantastic step forward and I applaud you. Remember, deep breathing doesn't require you to be sat in the lotus position with your eyes closed. No-one needs to know you're doing this and so feel free to do it wherever you are at the moment. Go on, give it a go!

Sleep

I get asked a lot what I think the number one thing is for our wellbeing, and I know people are expecting me to say something like eating plenty of vegetables or anything associated with nutrition, but my answer will always be sleep. It's so critical to how we feel and function on a daily basis.

People often think of sleep as a dormant state, but the reality is quite the opposite. It's a hugely active process and many critical functions take place whilst we are sleeping.

Sleep will support our learning, the formation of memories and the ability to retrieve them, emotional stability, blood sugar regulation, appetite regulation and weight management, digestive health, cardiovascular health and even our immunity. Think of all the things that can go awry if we're not sleeping. Despite how you're feeling from an emotional and energy perspective, long-term sleep deprivation is linked to mood swings, addictions, cravings, cardiovascular disease and even Alzheimer's Disease.

We know it's within our interests to have a good night's sleep but numerous studies report that we are getting less and less sleep than we did just a few decades ago. This is clearly a problem, but one that we can each individually choose to do something about.

Eight hours is often still reported as the optimal amount, but I tend to advise people not to get too hung up on that. If the optimal is eight and we're only getting five, the gap can seem too large and end up becoming a stressor in itself. If your sleep is not where you want it to be, my advice is to focus on getting a bit more than you are doing currently, even 15 minutes. Realistic goals are really important in this process.

Some top tips for maximising your chances of improved quantity and quality of sleep include:

- Getting plenty of daylight first thing in the morning and throughout the day, then minimising artificial light later in the evening, thereby encouraging a healthy sleep-wake hormonal rhythm.
- Taking time throughout the day to relax, absorb and process your thoughts so that your brain doesn't have to go into overdrive as you suddenly stop whilst climbing into bed.
- Consciously having wind-down time and making your evening free of stimulants – caffeine, sugar, alcohol (sorry!)
- Going tech-free at least an hour before bed, ideally longer. A very hard one I know, but getting rid of the blue light exposure from our screens and the stimulation from the content is important for sleep.
- Creating the right environment for sleep in the bedroom – dark, cool and without screens.
- And remember to breathe deeply as part of your routine!

I do absolutely understand that some of you may have more deep-rooted challenges with sleep and that, despite adopting all these habits and techniques, it still evades you. I also fully empathise with what that feels like; I struggled severely with my sleep for a number of years and felt the impact on my life, wellbeing, and well …. everything. If sleep is a real challenge and you're confident you have all the right things in place to encourage deep sleep, then seeking support is something I would encourage. It's an area I help clients with frequently and is often the first thing we will look at for all of the reasons described above.

My last word on sleep for now is that even if you're in bed and not sleeping, do your best to be accepting of that fact and take some comfort in the knowledge that you are resting. Getting yourself into that 'rest and digest' state through mindful or deep breathing should help you to stay calm and restful.

Rest

A subject very closely linked to sleep and the regular deep breathing, but something we don't do much of in our increasingly busy lives is the art of resting. It's not only that we no longer value time to rest and 'just be', but when we do have ten minutes we no longer seem to know how to rest and instead reach for our phones or some form of passive stimulation. I'm saddened by what I see when I look around me in public spaces, everyone head down on their phone. I'm not immune: unless I'm very conscious about it I'll do it myself – it's become such an ingrained habit enforced by what we observe around us.

We'll have the technology debate later, but right now I want to focus on the subject of resting. Do you ever just do nothing, nothing at all, even for five minutes? Or are you multitasking to the max every second of the day, being super time-efficient and not wasting a moment. Do you consider someone sitting and doing nothing to be lazy? Would you feel guilty if someone were to see you resting and doing nothing in your everyday routine?

It's interesting how, over time, we have celebrated and rewarded busy-ness to the extent of disparaging any form of relaxation, when it's such a critical contributor to our health, physically and mentally. In the context of resilience think very much about our cognitive function, brain and mental health. We require down-time (and off-time) in order to be able to process information and thoughts, to be able to make informed and sound decisions, to avoid making mistakes, and even to be present in the moment with the people around us.

So how do you begin to integrate some rest into your routine when you're already stretched? A great starting point is to deliberately avoid any distraction or stimulation when you'd normally mindlessly reach for your phone. This might be on a journey, standing in a queue, passing time whilst waiting for a friend to meet you for dinner, or any other time when it can feel slightly uncomfortable being alone. Instead, consciously be in the moment – people watch, let your mind wander freely and uncensored, pick out things you appreciate, or you could even do some deep breathing! Try it today and notice how it feels. It may immediately feel liberating and relaxing, but most likely it will feel uncomfortable to start with.

Ultimately it would be great to consistently have at least thirty minutes of rest during your normal busy day, enabling yourself to process and function better. This could simply be mindfully eating your lunch, rather than eating whilst working and checking your phone. See what you can do to rest today a little more than you did yesterday.

Hydration

Staying hydrated sounds so easy and simple, doesn't it? But unfortunately many of us are not keeping ourselves sufficiently hydrated. Water is the body's main component, making up at least half of our body weight, and playing a part in many functions such as digestion, detoxification, body temperature, helping send key messages around the body, and brain function. It's reported that even as little as 2% dehydration can start to impair our cognitive function – that in itself is a motivator for me!

We use and lose water through more than just urination - our breath, perspiration and also our bowel movements are ways that we excrete water. This water needs to be constantly replenished in order for us to remain hydrated at a cellular level. We take on water through drinking it directly and through other liquids, as well as through certain foods, particularly fruits and vegetables. Foods like watermelon, cucumber and spinach are more than 90% water content, for example.

The question I'm always being asked is "how much water should I be drinking?" It's not a straightforward answer as hydration needs vary according to a whole range of factors including age, gender, body mass, health, nutrition, temperature and activity levels. Even pregnancy and breast-feeding will influence our requirements. Nevertheless in my quest to keep it simple, my advice for any adult is:

- An absolute minimum of two litres of water, sipped gradually over the whole course of the day, rather than being gulped down in one go.
- Increase this as soon as you're in a hot climate, are doing lots of activity, are experiencing more perspiration than normal, or have a health status that requires more hydration.
- The best rule of thumb is that your hydration is OK if you rarely feel thirsty and your urine is colourless or light yellow.

Finding ways to always have access to a drink of water sounds simple, but is what a lot of people struggle with. So definitely think about how to make this easy for yourself in your routine, whether that's a flask of water with you in the car, always filling your glass whenever you make a hot drink, or keeping several glasses on the go around the house. Make it easy for yourself.

Lastly, if you're a big tea or coffee drinker it can be helpful to implement a 'water chaser' habit, simply referring to having a glass of water between any drinks that can dehydrate such as tea, coffee and alcohol.

Nutrition

This is an emotional and confusing subject for many people. There are libraries of books on the subject, there are countless diets everywhere you turn, there are slimming clubs galore, there are new insights being reported all the time which may contradict what we've previously understood, and there is always conflict, even between the experts. Quite often clients will say to me, "I'm so confused, I just need you to tell me what to eat and I'll do it!"

As a Nutritional Therapist I understand the immense power and influence food has on our physical and mental health, our sense of wellbeing and vibrancy, our longevity, and our levels of resilience. I have created hundreds of nutritional protocols to support clients to achieve their goals, and what I've learned in doing that, is that the simpler we can keep things, the more likely it is that someone can implement and maintain change in amongst their busy life, and subsequently feel the benefits.

People often ask me my opinion of the 'best' diet – vegan, vegetarian, paleo, high protein, high fat, low carb, fasting protocols, and so on. Some people may disagree with me, particularly those steadfast on particular eating regimes, but my answer is always along the lines of "whatever is right for you". I know that might be a frustrating response, but like everything I'll talk about in this book, the right answer is always more personal than that.

You'll have gathered that I'm somewhat of a pragmatist rather than a purist in my approach to nutrition and wellbeing. Whilst there might be a wealth of evidence around a specific diet, if it's difficult to implement into your life, then what's the point in me recommending it? You'll just end up with a sense of failure and no further forward than you were before. My role is to understand the whole you, to be able to present you with options that could work, and together we choose a way forward.

What I'm going to share with you in this book are some general principles that I believe can serve anyone confused about food, and you'll discover that the majority of the recommendations aren't even about the food itself!

- Connect with your food – as a result of the vast confusion around food, the need to be told what to eat rather than decide for ourselves, the desire for things to be quick to fit in with our lives and the mass of convenience in the food industry, we have become increasingly disconnected with how we nourish ourselves through food. It's a real problem. So first things first, we need to consciously connect with our nutrition through mindful eating.
- Understand your needs – a key part of this is rediscovering the art of tuning in to our bodies and hearing the signals it so clearly sends us. If we've been disconnected from our food for a long time, often due to long-term dieting, this can take some

time to develop. Just start by asking yourself what food will nourish you and enable you to feel your best right now, and listen to the answer.

- Mindful eating – because we're so often in a rush, multi-tasking or eating on the go, we can eat in a mindless way, involving little to zero connection with our food. Use all of your senses when thinking about your food, when preparing it, and especially when eating it. Give your meal your undivided attention and be mindful how it makes you feel before, during and after. When we eat mindfully our amazingly intelligent body can digest much more effectively, thereby allowing us to optimise the nourishment we gain.

- Avoid food rules – I know, this is controversial! Nevertheless, I'm really keen that we all avoid what I refer to as food rules. You can do this, you must never do that, this is good, this is bad, I'm allowed this, I've been good so I can have this, it's best to eat at this time, and so on. It we connect, truly tune in to what we need and makes us feel great, and eat mindfully, then we can guide ourselves to the answer.

- Recognise your needs change – whether this be due to stress, different life stages or ill-health, it's important to recognise that our nutritional needs can change. Another reason for constantly being able to tune in.

I suspect that sounds like an unachievable list for many of you, and I understand that. It takes some work. But that's why I do have a few guiding principles to help you with your choices. Before you read them, promise me you'll really consider whether they *feel* right for you and why/why not. That intuition will help inform your future choices.

The list is deliberately short:

- Choose foods that are whole, natural, fresh and unprocessed – they will have the greatest potential to nourish you.
- Max out on your vegetables and fruit – they are packed tightly with nutrients that will serve you well.
- Enjoy all the food groups – carbohydrates, fats and proteins in the proportions that you find help you feel vibrant.
- Minimise substances that can act as stressors for the body to digest and detoxify – sugar, caffeine, toxins, anything artificial and processed.

Just to emphasise – these are not strict rules – they are simple guidelines to inform your choices. But more important than any of these is your ability to use mindfulness and your intuition around how you nourish yourself with food.

There is one distinction that I will make; a time when stricter food protocols do come into play. When someone is dealing with chronic ill-health it often represents an imbalance of one or more systems of the body. To help re-balance those systems and improve health we can intelligently use nutrition to support this process. In those circumstances, recommendations are more targeted and strict, but with a clear longer term goal in mind that also allows flexibility again.

Nutrition can be complex and confusing; my role is to make it simple and accessible for the person in front of me. With my qualifications and expertise I can guide and inform, but ultimately my role is to coach and support you to make the changes that will make a difference in your life.

Movement

As a society we have advanced so much to make our lives easier, more convenient and more accessible, yet whilst doing so other challenges have been created. Becoming an increasingly sedentary generation is one of them. We are sitting now more than we have ever done – when travelling, at our desks for work, even modern day leisure activities such as watching TV, going to the cinema or a restaurant, and the likes.

A phrase that really caught on in the media recently was "sitting is the new smoking" where it was reported that our sedentary lives carry as many health risks as smoking. Whilst the science around that assertion has been questioned, I consider it wise to take heed of the sentiment of the statement. We weren't meant to sit for the significant majority of the time; we were designed to move naturally throughout the day as a core part of our survival.

The benefits of movement are substantial to overall health and can also be of benefit to stress management. Fitness and strength make us less prone to injury (unless we're moving in the wrong way!), oxygen and nutrients quickly reach places they need to via the bloodstream, our lung capacity can improve, it can help with weight management, and the mental health benefits are considered substantial. Physical movement can certainly leave us with the feel-good factor due to the release of neurotransmitters called endorphins. All of this can lead us to the very logical conclusion that all exercise is good for us, and the most recent evidence base and trend is for short bursts of high intensity training.

Something often omitted from discussions on exercise is that more intense exercises can act as a stressor, stimulating the release or cortisol and adrenaline. If you think about it, there is logic in that. If we're doing something extreme such as high intensity interval training (HIIT) then that would be perceived as a stressor by the body and in order to perform to your best in that situation you'll need the boost provided by stress hormones. That's another reason that these forms of exercise can leave you buzzing and on high alert for a short period.

Given that this is a book about stress and the quest to avoid burnout, it's only right for me to issue a word a caution in amongst all the continued excitement around HIIT forms of exercise. If you are already experiencing chronic stress and potentially heading towards burnout, then it could be the case that any form of very intense activity could leave you feeling rotten. The last thing you need is another hit of stress hormones flooding your system. You might get a very short term lift, but then be left feeling exhausted with nothing left. It can even leave some people feeling quite poorly.

You know what's coming! The key is to tune in to what's right for you at the time. Yes, we want and need to do some form of movement, but if your best friend is pushing you to a HIIT class when you know a yoga class would serve you better, trust your intuition. You do know what's best.

The people I work with who have experienced burnout do also tend to be the type who will be drawn to something intense. Like everything in life, there's a need to get the most benefit in the shortest amount of time and high intensity looks like it ticks those boxes. If you know undertaking that form of exercise does you the world of good, then keep doing it. If, however, it leaves you feeling significantly less than your best, it's time to try something else for a while.

The other thing to remember is that this section is referred to as movement, rather than exercise, quite deliberately. We need to move our bodies but that doesn't have to mean putting on your lycra and heading to the gym to lift weights. It can mean doing some stretching at home, taking a walk, going out on your bike, gardening, attending a pilates class, housework, any manner of activity that involves you moving.

Taking us back to an earlier chapter I would also encourage you to engage in movement that doubles up as a moment of joy. We all have limited time, so why not do something you really enjoy, that makes you feel great, that nourishes you and, in turn, helps generate resilience?

Movement is a key part of both wellbeing and resilience and something I would highly encourage on a daily basis. My advice is to do something every day no matter how small, to mix it up, to ensure it's something that you enjoy and helps you feel really great.

Address Ill-Health

When thinking about nourishing your body the last thing I want to cover is the need to address any area of ill-health that you are experiencing. For lots of reasons we put up with what I refer to as low-grade illnesses – things that don't have an enormous impact, so we just leave them and get on with our busy day. We certainly wouldn't think of going to our doctor with it.

This could be as simple as frequently getting a cold, sore throat or mouth ulcers, being tired all the time, having a fungal toenail, or having constant digestive upset, for example. Having a low-grade illness uses up vital resources such as energy and nutrients. It can also prompt a constant low-level stress response as we're dealing with an ongoing infection. Ultimately it's adding to the stress load.

Our body is giving us a sign and we can choose to listen and respond in a way that will benefit us for a long time, or we can ignore it by taking action to numb it and crack on with our to-do list. I know which I did for many years when I considered being ill an enormous inconvenience. Where are you on this scale currently?

If you're feeling unwell, focus on giving your body what it needs, usually rest and nutrients. If it's persistent then seek help rather than ignore it – no matter how busy you are. Consider it one of your early warning signs.

Do Any Of These Areas Warrant Your Attention?

I'm all about small and achievable steps to provide an enhanced chance of success, progress and motivation. In this chapter we've covered the subjects of breathing, sleeping, resting, hydrating, moving, nutrition and addressing ill-health. Is there an area, or even one aspect of one of these areas, that you would benefit from looking at?

8

NOURISH YOUR MIND

The power of our thoughts, beliefs and overall mindset is crucial to our outlook on life, the way we approach situations, how we feel, our ambitions and sense of achievement, and so much more. Adopting practices and habits that nourish our mind is just as key as any other area for building resilience. I'm sure many would argue it's the most important aspect; personally I'd say that depends on the individual and what their needs are at the time.

I'm going to take you through a few subjects that consistently have a positive impact with a whole range of clients. All are simple, free and accessible, yet they are all things many of us neglect because we are hurrying through our day. They can be the first things to forget, when really they should be amongst the things that we always protect.

I will remind you of my earlier disclaimer – I'm not a mindset or mental health professional such as a psychologist, psychotherapist, clinical hypnotherapist, NLP practitioner, or the like. I do however have a deep interest and strong belief in the power of our minds when it comes to managing stress, building resilience and creating the path that allows us to have it all.

I first want to remind you about your 'moments of joy'. The whole concept is centred around focusing on the many positive experiences we have, no matter how small, and then working towards replicating those moments as much as possible. I won't repeat it all here; I simply want to jog your memory. Take a step back to chapter 5 if you want a recap.

Clear Purpose

I wrote about your 'why' earlier in this section because it's important to understand the drivers influencing your actions and the way you are living your life. The ideal scenario is for our actions, experiences and achievements to align with our 'why'. Many people would refer to this as their purpose in life, and in certain situations that language would be more fitting and comfortable for people to use.

Having a clear understanding of your purpose is important for understanding and managing stress, and therefore for building resilience. I've read many times in professional texts and publications that those who have a clear purpose in their life tend to have a more positive and optimistic outlook, that they are often able to overcome obstacles more easily, and can recover from adversity quicker. Doesn't this sound like the definition of resilience?

What I have observed for myself, with friends and family, and with clients is that the greater the clarity of purpose for someone:

- The clearer they are on their priorities and how they spend their time.
- The greater their focus and the less they get distracted with things that are misaligned.
- The more time they appear to have for what brings them joy, because they aren't saying 'yes' to the volume of requests and suggestions that come their way.
- The more persistent and tenacious they are in overcoming challenges that could prevent them from achieving their goal.
- The people around them have a clearer understanding of that person's identity, purpose and values.

There are so many benefits available to us from having this clarity – resilience, time, focus, energy and motivation, to name but a few. If you're already clear on this, then move forward and keep checking that your actions and focus are aligned. If they are not, then simply take one small step closer each day.

Technology Switch Off

I know this is a controversial one, likely sending shivers down your spine – I promise you, it does the same to me too. But that doesn't mean we should avoid the subject (sorry!).

The brain absolutely must have downtime if it is to be effective at problem solving, creating memories, being able to make good decisions, and to essentially have good cognitive function. Yet we are keeping our brains 'on' all the time in a state of maximum stimulation through the constant use of technology. How many of you watch TV whilst also checking your phone, maybe even with a laptop or tablet on your knee, whilst supposedly spending time with your family? How effective do you feel you are at any of the things you are trying to give your attention to?

Many of us have grown up in the era of multi-tasking being a much sought-after and complimented skill. Completing multiple tasks simultaneously, ensuring we minimise any downtime or spare capacity. Never leaving a moment unproductive. Whilst I'm not saying the concept isn't valid for certain activities, I am certain that it wasn't intended for multiple simultaneous activities requiring a concentrated cerebral focus. Yet that's what we're doing. Just not very well.

The term single-tasking has come to the fore in recent years, promoting the fact that certain activities require a singular uninterrupted focus to achieve the best results. I know that when I'm writing or developing creative content I need to have my phone switched off along with all the notifications that can ping across my laptop screen. It's the only way for me to be productive. If I don't, the constant distractions will throw me off course, reduce my productivity and creativity, and cause a level of frustration with my lack of progress.

Do you have a good understanding of how and when you are most effective, and how technology helps or hinders? It's worthy of exploration, for yourself but also for family members and colleagues.

In addition to all of this there's the reported health risks around EMFs (ElectroMagnetic Fields) associated with all wireless devices and transmissions; some would say all electronic devices. I know the subject of EMFs and health risks is still a controversial topic. Personally I believe the risks to be real and something to be taken note of; although I'm deliberately not going into that debate here and will let you do your own research.

In an age where we depend on our personal technology for just about everything, I have a few recommendations for you to consider in order to prevent technology being a stressor and weakening your resilience.

- Consciously and mindfully engage with your technology when you have a purpose for doing so; try and avoid the mindless default setting of reaching for your phone when you are bored or have a minute to spare.

- Start the day on your own terms by avoiding your device being the first thing you look at in the morning. When you wake, allow yourself at least a little time before you look (ideally quite a bit of time). As soon as you look at that screen in a morning your thoughts and agenda for the day are being hijacked by someone else.
- Finish the day on your terms and give your brain time to wind down by leaving that same device alone before bed.
- Remove unnecessary notifications, both visual and auditory. You don't need to know that someone has just added something to their Instagram story whilst you're in a meeting at work or having dinner with your family. The constant distraction not only affects your performance, but also your relationships.
- Have some off-time every day.

You'll have your own ideas too. I believe the key is to focus on staying a master of your technology, rather than becoming a slave to it.

Mindfulness

The mindfulness movement and industry is enormous and continues to grow; a response to the way in which we are increasingly living our lives which has the potential to leave us stressed, overwhelmed and unwell. It's such a simple and powerful approach to life, encouraging us to be present in the moment and accepting of our thoughts and feelings, whatever they may be.

The link to resilience is that it enables us to slow down, experience joy in the moment, deal with our emotions in a positive way, and can help shift our nervous system into a more relaxed state. It is widely accepted as a stress-reducing activity and approach to life. Mindfulness can apply to any situation and experience. Already in this book I've referred to mindful breathing and mindful eating. I'm sure you can easily think of situations when you are not as present as you'd like to be, or you could benefit from calming body and mind in order to experience the moment.

If you're new to the subject of mindfulness and feel like this could be for you, then I'd highly encourage you to look for an introductory class in your area, check out some reading material, or download an app. But before all of that you can simply choose one scenario in which you commit to be mindful. Let's say that's eating dinner with your family – all distractions are off and away, allowing you the opportunity to sit, eat and enjoy the moment. Don't force anything, just let it be and accept whatever feelings come up. Use all of your senses and relish the experience.

Meditation

The art of meditative practice is an ancient tradition with history, rituals and techniques that I certainly couldn't do justice to. It's often misunderstood as an activity you are required to do perfectly and should complete for an extended period of time each day. I don't believe perfection and rules are part of what meditation is about. For me, meditation is a form of training for the mind, enabling greater focus, clarity and calm. The reported benefits of meditation are broad – reducing stress, reducing anxiety, improving mental and emotional health, improving cognitive functions such as memory and concentration, improving sleep, and even helping to control pain.

I know from personal experience that on the days I do meditate (and my meditation is usually no more than five minutes) I have a deeper sense of focus and clarity. It's as though the practice has allowed an entire cart of mental clutter to be cleared away.

Of course, we all want to know how much we should do, what the optimal amount is. There are reports that between 12-15 minutes daily is the minimum to enjoy all of the physical and mental health benefits available. Whilst that doesn't sound a long time I do know that for many of my clients who are struggling to even find the time to go to the bathroom between meetings, this might be a step too far as a starting point. That's why I tend to begin with a suggestion of deep breathing for just a minute at a time. Small steps are all it takes to see a difference.

There are hundreds, if not thousands, of meditation apps out there. If you're new to meditation and want to try it then having a guided meditation is often the chosen way forward. I will only do a guided meditation; my thoughts are too busy otherwise. Once I've found the right voice, rhythm and duration, then I'm good to go. If you can find a way to integrate it into your day, even for five minutes, I know you'll enjoy the benefits.

Gratitude & Appreciation

A daily focus on what we are grateful for is another simple but highly effective technique for focusing on the positive, and in doing so, de-prioritising the negative. A regular gratitude practice is said to have benefits for our physical and mental health, our relationships, and our levels of resilience.

I honestly don't think it could be easier. Spend a few minutes daily to acknowledge what you are grateful for, no matter how small and simple. Or list three things in a morning and three things at night. Or spend the time you are waiting in a queue to reflect on what you appreciate about the situation rather than reach for your phone. It could be a blue sky, the kindness of a stranger, completing a project you've been working on for ages, a message from a friend, your train being on time, a flower coming into bloom, a nice cup of tea – the list is endless. Simplicity is often the key.

For clients that are also parents, this can become a family ritual at some point in the day, usually at the dinner table or at bedtime, amplifying the benefits as all the gratitude is shared.

Make Your Peace

I'm sure all of us have had the experience of being angry and frustrated at a person or a situation; feeling stressed due to the actions of others and powerless in our ability to do anything about it. We may end up holding a grudge, sometimes for long periods of time. In doing so, we extend the duration in which we are experiencing negative emotion and the associated stress responses.

Are there certain things you think about which still make your blood boil, immediately prompting those feelings again? When I was living life at a hundred miles an hour in high pressure environments, I frequently found myself getting agitated by things I didn't like or agree with. They would sit with me for too long and if my mind wandered onto that subject I would easily become stressed about it again. I didn't have the capacity or the inclination to make my peace with it, to forgive and move on.

I see this trait commonly in clients I'm working with that are experiencing extreme stress. Making your peace takes time, energy and a sense of calm or stillness. It's a reflective practice making it a difficult thing to achieve when you're living life at pace. The consequence tends to be that you are carrying more stress than you need to, which means there's an opportunity to release some of that heavy load.

Remember that making your peace with someone or a situation doesn't mean condoning or excusing; it is simply your decision to consciously let it go, to be free of all the negative associations, and to focus on moving yourself forward positively. Talking about it, writing it down, and committing the time to work it through are all helpful strategies. Whatever the right way forward for you, I'd encourage you to not let something like a grudge take up any more of your energy. It's a liberating achievement.

Journaling

Many of us can find the prospect of journaling a bit daunting. There's a blank piece of paper – what are you supposed to write about? In my day, journaling was simply referred to as writing in your diary, during which we were encouraged to write about our day, including anything that had gone well and thoughts that were a worry. It was a private space, just meant for you and your thoughts. If you ever kept a diary, then you already know how to journal. There are no rules. It's a personal and uncensored place. Let the pen flow and reap the rewards.

The benefits from journaling are widespread, and which I personally summarise as helping you to keep a clear and healthy mind. The act of writing in such a freeing way can help with mental de-cluttering, sorting through thoughts and problems, increasing self-awareness, helping provide clarity whilst also giving you insights to patterns and connections.

You don't need anything other than a pen and paper. I've even journaled on the back of a used envelope! Nevertheless, if a blank piece of paper gives you writer's block then you can buy a guided journal where you are prompted to answer certain questions to help you reflect on your day.

Does Your Mind Need Nourishing?

If you're at the point where you're struggling to focus, you can't think straight or you frequently experience brain fog then it's highly likely your mind could do with a bit of attention and support. The areas covered in this chapter are intended to be quick and easy; why not choose one and give it a go?

9

NOURISH FOR CONNECTION

Y ou will have heard the phrase many times – we're more connected than we've ever been, yet also the most isolated. The influences of spending time behind a screen, spending more hours at work and living life at a fast pace are all contributing to a breakdown in real human connection. As human beings we have a need for meaningful and deep connection in order to feel well, vibrant, healthy and able to handle what comes our way.

Loneliness is associated with sizeable emotional and physical health risks and a recent UK study by the British Red Cross revealed that over nine million adults in the UK are either always or often lonely – that's the equivalent of nearly everyone that lives in London.

Being connected doesn't just mean being in contact with others; it means having a connection or relationship that recognises and appreciates who you really are. All too often

I hear friends and clients talk about being surrounded by people all day, but with a sense of isolation due to a disconnect. I've experienced it myself, particularly when I was becoming unwell with something I didn't understand and therefore couldn't explain.

Real Connection

The key here is to ensure that you are experiencing real connection on a daily basis, and for some that can be a sizeable challenge. My hope is that you have people in your life that you feel relaxed around, where you can just be yourself without fear of judgement, to whom you can talk to about anything, and with whom you smile and laugh.

They don't have to be your life-long best friend; it can just as easily be a trusted colleague at the office. Whoever they are, they're the ones to spend the majority of your time with, to seek out when you need support, and to proactively invest your efforts in. These are the people you want to be spending most of your time with!

Due to the advances in technology lots of people can now work from home, opening opportunities and flexibility to many who wouldn't have had it otherwise. I work from home and consider it a real privilege, although it does come with some downsides, one being that you spend an increasing amount of time alone. Clients often fall into this category too and so I wanted to touch on it.

If you predominantly work from home it's important to consider ways in which you can get some real connection during the working day. This can be as simple as a walk to the local coffee shop, or choosing a day to go to a co-working space, or having a work buddy that you always check in with daily, or attending networking events. The solution for you will depend on what you do for a living, but if you have a sense of isolation through work then let people know and explore your options. If you're feeling that way, it's likely that some of your colleagues are too.

Given my very happy and fulfilling co-existence with my dog Lexi, it would be remiss of me to exclude the real and deep connection that we can have with our pets in this section. The bond is powerful and whilst we might not speak the same language, the connection can be a lifeline for some. Therapy animals are increasing in use and there are now countless studies reporting the benefits for mental health. So there you go, if you prefer animals to humans you're probably in good hands (paws!).

Mood Hoovers & Energy Vampires

Just like there are people whom you connect with and whose energy always provide you with a lift and a boost, there are those people who do the opposite. The people who somehow sap all of your energy and leave your mood in the doldrums. They seem to have lost their zest and radiate a constant sense of negativity. No matter how positive you are, they can obliterate your good vibe mo-jo in one conversation.

It goes without saying that these are not your people. It doesn't mean they are bad or wrong, they're simply not the right match for you at this point in time. Nevertheless, if you're regularly affected by a mood hoover or energy vampire then your resilience will undoubtedly be impacted. If it is possible, they are people to minimise your exposure to for the time being. If they are one of your nearest and dearest then I appreciate that's a bit more difficult, and I'd encourage some open discussion (along with a bit of deep breathing).

If it feels appropriate, then practising compassion with this person is always a good option. I don't mean indulging the negative outlook, but working to understand what might be driving it. You never know, a bit of support and coaching from you could make all the difference.

If spending regular time with a mood hoover is a given for you, then work to ensure that the rest of your time is surrounded by positivity and uplifting people – you'll know who they are!

Kindness

I think we all enjoy being on the receiving end of kindness and most of us get some real satisfaction from offering kindness to others. It creates connection, it helps keep spirits high, it can be a mood booster and help with self-esteem, and most of us would say it just feels good.

Now, I may be stretching the direct link to resilience with this one, but I honestly believe in its value for this purpose. Kindness is known to create moments of joy, to improve relationships along with a sense of connection and community. And let's face it, kindness is pretty contagious. When you're on the receiving end of kindness you're more likely to pay it forward. If a fellow driver lets you out into traffic, do you become more likely to do the same for another?

In my mind, kindness is most powerful when it's in the moment, simple and usually free. Holding the door open, complimenting someone's appearance, saying thank you, offering to help someone who appears to be struggling, having a conversation with someone who strikes you as lonely, giving up your seat on public transport, or simply being helpful in a time of need. Of course, bigger gestures fall into this category too, the more thoughtful the better.

When we're very busy it can be easy to side-step an opportunity to be kind, but why not try to do something daily and see how it feels?

My motto on this subject: offer kindness willingly and receive graciously – it's such a beautiful part of the human spirit.

Hug It Out

I know not everyone is a 'hugger' and that hugs are not appropriate in all situations; in fact, they may get you into trouble in some! Just know that a big hug for a good duration can stimulate the release of hormones that help us feel calm and safe, therefore shifting the nervous system into the relaxed state we are aiming for. There's a reason we instinctively hug someone when they are upset or frightened.

I've seen many work environments where hugs are commonplace and others where it's definitely not the done thing. Similarly, some family members enjoy a hug and others keep you at arm's length. It's not for everyone, but if you like a hug let others know that it's good for your health and 'hug it out'!

Laughter

You will have no doubt heard the saying *"laughter is the best medicine"* and there's real truth in that. The act of laughing, and even more so a good old belly laugh, stimulates the release of those feel-good chemicals that can have a distinct impact on our mood and outlook. I always used to say that one of the secrets to my happiness was at least one belly laugh a day, and I still stand by that.

Of course we can laugh alone, but for the majority of people it is something we do when we are connected with others.

Usually people we know, but sometimes we laugh with strangers too. And I imagine there's not many better ways to bring people together. It is one of those contagious actions – we can easily catch it and then find it hard to shake off.

If you know what raises the corners of your mouth and develops into a good hearty laugh, I would encourage you to get a dose of that as soon as possible.

Connecting Through Technology

I know, this may sound somewhat contradictory after I've just been going on and on about downtime from our devices. Nevertheless, this falls into using technology intentionally and for our overall wellbeing and resilience. Just as connection through technology can be superficial, it can also be meaningful and touching when used in the right way.

If a digital message or phone/video call is the only thing available to you right now in order to connect with the people who keep you energised, positive and lifted, then by all means go for it. I would still argue that the in-person connection is always most effective, however I know I can feel on top of the world after a quick call with the right person, and I'm sure you can too.

How Connected Are You Feeling?

Be honest with yourself. Do you feel well connected at a level that supports your wellbeing and resilience? If yes, how do you think you can help others feel more connected? If not, are there any of these suggestions that could help you?

10

ENVIRONMENT THAT NOURISHES

D o you notice how your surroundings make you feel? Do you ever choose a specific environment to help you complete a task or to meet a certain need that you have? Do you observe how other people respond differently to the same environment? Consciously or unconsciously, I'm certain you will make choices about the environment you put yourself in, likely several times a day.

Matching our needs with the right environment that can be a simple and powerful technique for keeping stress levels down. For example, if I've a deadline to meet for writing a presentation that requires me to achieve deep concentration and focus then I would normally opt for complete silence and zero distractions or interruptions. Whereas if I need an energy and creativity boost for a different type of project I would choose a more bustling environment with some uplifting music; soaking up the sights and sounds would help me.

Think about your family and circle of friends and think about the times you've said things like:

- I enjoy going to visit where they live, but I couldn't live there, it's too busy and noisy.
- I enjoy going to visit where they live, but I couldn't live there, it's too quiet with nothing to do.
- I don't know how they can function with all of that clutter around.
- I can't relax there, with everything so neat and tidy.
- I can't think straight with all of that noise.
- I can't think straight in the silence.

You get the idea. As with every subject we are covering, the environment we need for thriving is personal to us, and the more aware we are of our needs and how to achieve them, the better our resilience will be.

Let's explore some of the common factors that can directly influence how we feel and our ability to manage stress.

Green Space

I fully realise I'm a little biased here as there's not much I enjoy more than spending time in the great outdoors, usually walking with my dog Lexi. It quickly and easily brings me a sense of peace, appreciation and enjoyment.

Second to deep breathing it's my quickest route to de-stress. Not only can I reach a sense of calm, I also find it enhances my creativity and problem solving – an added bonus!

But this isn't unique to me. There are studies that highlight how time in green space and with nature can contribute positively to our mental health and overall wellbeing. I'm yet to come across anyone who doesn't find it calming and beneficial for reducing stress.

It doesn't have to mean getting your hiking kit on and heading out on the nearest footpath through fields. It can be some time in your local park, working on your allotment, sitting in the garden, visiting a garden open to the public, trying to integrate a park on your walk to the office, having a view of some green space from your window, even having a picture of green space or a plant on your desk.

When I decided to base myself from a home office, one thing really important to me was to have clear views of my garden and ideally some countryside beyond. It was part of my criteria for buying a house when I moved, knowing how important it was to my wellbeing.

When I lived and worked in a city, I had to work harder to achieve the same results, yet I managed to see some green space on my walk from the public transport stop in a morning, and I would get down to the local river bank for a stroll in the evening and at weekends. There is always a way.

Light

I could have easily put this subject in the Body or Mind sections given the very close link to subjects like sleep, relaxation and the ability to switch off. We need exposure to natural light to keep our sleep-wake cycle in rhythm for quality sleep, sunlight to our skin (even through the clouds) is critical for Vitamin D levels, and for those who experience Seasonal Affective Disorder (SAD) natural light is a must.

Many of us now spend a lot of time in buildings that use artificial light, and we are also staring at a multitude of screens which is not only artificial, but is referred to as 'blue light' that can really interfere with the sleep-wake cycle. In the UK we have several months of the year where we are travelling to and from work in the dark, reducing the opportunity for natural light.

The use of light may not seem the most obvious factor for building resilience, but work in a windowless office for forty hours a week during the winter and see how you feel then. It really does make a difference.

Increase your exposure to natural light as much as possible by considering:

- Taking your breaks outside and ensuring you get regular access to daylight through the working day.
- Choose to exercise in a natural environment or opt

for a gym that has access to plenty of windows and feels bright.

- When indoors, especially in an office building, spend as much time as possible near windows.
- A more in-depth measure at home includes choosing window dressings that not only maximise your light during the day, but also provide the darkness that's necessary at night time.

For those who do experience SAD, then the therapeutic use of a light box from mid-autumn through late-winter can certainly be beneficial. Get advice on how best to use as over exposure can cause a different issue.

Noise

This is one of the areas I tend to find most individual difference with. There are people who appear to thrive when surrounded by lots of noise and all the hustle and bustle that goes with it, and others who predominantly prefer a quiet space. Whilst we might have a favourite kind of music, we will also have a variety to suit different moods and needs.

The use of noise and sound is very powerful and my suggestion is that you use it to your advantage. The range of emotions evoked through this sense are hugely varied – calming, relaxing, upsetting, frustrating, annoying, uplifting, energising, exciting, and many more.

Consider the noise associated with the environments in the different parts of your life and reflect on what works well for you and why – work, home, transport, leisure, social, for example. By tuning in to what helps you thrive in those different environments, the better you will be at managing any stressors.

Clutter

One of the hot topics of the moment is undoubtedly the de-cluttering movement; freeing our homes and work spaces of unnecessary clutter in order to help liberate the mind and help us think and live more freely. It makes sense, doesn't it? A clear desk whilst we are working keeps us focused on the one thing we should be doing right now, and as a result we'll get it done quicker and more effectively. A home free of the surplus makes it easier to clean and find things!

I have a confession to make here as I'm a bit of a paradox. I don't like clutter. I completely buy in to the need to de-clutter and all of the benefits associated. Yet I also have a lot of stuff, much of it not needed anymore. It's all away in cupboards and the house and office are largely tidy and neat. However, the clutter behind doors still takes up some mental space as I think of all the sorting out I should do. I'm sure I'm an ideal client for a professional de-clutterer!

If the pile of papers, mountain of washing, overloaded inbox, or drawer of old chargers cause you distraction and a bit of angst each time you see them, then it's arguably time to do something about it. Start with something small and see if it helps lighten the load. If it does, choose the next category. If not, don't worry about it.

Keep it Clean

I'm not talking here about making your environment 99.9% free of all known germs, that's another debate entirely. What I am referring to is reducing the exposure to chemicals and toxins that can cause the body additional stress due to the need to detoxify. We can't eliminate toxins from our lives entirely, so please don't make that your goal. Rather focus on small, easy things you can do to reduce the toxic load.

For example, this could include:

- Consuming organic fruit and vegetables where available and when you can afford.
- Using more natural cleaning products and detergents.
- Choosing foods free of artificial preservatives.
- Spending more time in green space where the air is typically cleaner.
- Even opting for toxin-free paints next time you decorate at home.

This is a big subject and can sometimes be a frightening read when you start plugging this subject into your search engine. Don't allow it to be a stressor; simply choose one thing to try and do differently if this area is important to you.

Do You Need To Spruce Up Your Environment?

Given the subjects we've covered, do you feel that making some small changes to your environment would help you to thrive more and feel increasingly resilient? It's a broad subject and you may likely think of other subjects I haven't covered. Whatever you believe will help you feel less stressed, opt for that first.

11

NOURISH YOUR TIME

This has to be the biggest obstacle of all – time! More specifically, the lack of time to fit everything in and tick each item off the to-do list. How many times do you say those words on a daily basis? I don't have the time. I don't know where I'll find the time. I'll just have to make more time.

We can't buy or conjure up more time. We all have the same 24 hours in a day and no more. So what can we do? Extend our days by limiting sleep? Extend our working days by sacrificing an hour at the gym? Make difficult choices between time for yourself and time for your family? Everything just feels like one big compromise and many people feel a big dose of guilt associated with the choices they are making.

Those people who suffer with burnout are often the people who don't want to make those sacrifices or difficult choices, or more accurately they don't know how to do so and still feel good about themselves. I well and truly fell into this camp. I haven't yet had a client who hasn't felt the pressure associated with the scarcity of time.

Not everyone seems to have this issue though. Those are the people to watch, learn from, and who have usually mastered the sections in this chapter. What we'll cover may at first appear ruthless or selfish, especially to any high achieving, people-pleasing perfectionists out there. As a result, they can be the hardest to implement. Yet without them, you will struggle to implement any of the things already covered in this section.

Self First

Yes, you've read that right. You have to come first. Before your partner, your parents, your friends, your colleagues, your neighbour, and even your children. You will have probably heard the phrase 'you can't pour from an empty cup' and that's exactly what this is about. If you continually put everyone else's needs before your own then you will likely end up burning out.

I know what I'm saying may feel completely unrealistic, even unpalatable, to many of you. We've been taught to put others first, that sacrificing our own needs for the benefit of others is the right thing to do, and that putting our own needs first is selfish. Nevertheless, I'm sure that guidance was never intended as an encouragement to sacrifice your own health and happiness.

In order to be able to give your very best to serving others, you need to be on top form yourself. When you're exhausted and agitated I'm pretty sure you won't be giving your children the best you can. When your cup is full then you're able to give of yourself in a whole different way.

You'll be starting to get a sense of what really nourishes you. Whether that's something you already do, or something new to try. That's what you need to be filling your cup with.

Let's be realistic and pragmatic with all of this. If you have two toddlers hanging off your leg whilst you're cleaning your teeth and trying to make them breakfast, then it's unlikely that you can take 90 minutes for a long countryside walk in the morning. However, you could do some basic deep breathing or be sure you have a nourishing lunch. The key is to know what works for you, what's easy to implement, and create that routine and habit.

Saying No

How many times have you ended up in a situation that's left you thinking … How have I ended up doing this? Why have I agreed to be here when I don't even enjoy it? Did I just commit to doing that again? How can I tell them I don't want to do this anymore? Yes, I have too, more times than I'd care to remember.

It's hard for many people to say no, especially when being asked for help by someone you care about, or a request from your manager at work, or being asked to do something for a good cause. Yet if the consequences are making sacrifices to your health and in your personal life, then surely it requires some thought.

My advice is to focus on four basic questions:

- What brings you joy?
- What is most important to you?
- What nourishes you?
- What are your goals?

If how you are spending your time doesn't contribute to any of these, then I would suggest it is time to make a change.

Of course I appreciate that choice isn't always in our gift. If you're doing a job you don't enjoy you can't suddenly stop performing your duties without the risk of losing your only income stream. However, you can start taking action to make change, and that in itself should be satisfying – as long as it's moving towards ticking one of those questions above.

Deciding to say no is one thing, doing it is entirely different. For some it's an easy logical conversation, for others it's tangled up with feelings of guilt and worry. To make it easier, start telling people that you're feeling stretched too thin and are going to have to cut down on some commitments – it helps set the scene and enables others to empathise with what you're doing.

Time To Get Up

Due to grogginess or, increasingly, due to reaching for our phones as soon as we open our eyes, we're no longer getting out of bed when we first wake up or as soon as the alarm goes off. An extended period of scrolling on the phone or multiple snoozes can leave us feeling rushed and flustered before the day has even begun. And if you've spent half an hour on your phone whilst lying in bed, your mind has already been hijacked with everyone else's thoughts and agendas.

You might need a few moments to come to when you wake up, but getting up as soon as you can and investing a few minutes in a nourishing activity will set you up for a much better day. A meditation, some deep breathing, journaling, gentle stretching, a short exercise session – whichever works for you will undoubtedly lead you into a better day than reading the news, scrolling social media, or playing a game on your phone.

So it's an easy and short message. Give yourself the opportunity to nourish in a morning and when it's time to get up, get up. For many people I work with, this can easily be a 30-

minute window to help yourself have the best start to the day. Forming the habit is always the hardest, but my assurance is you will feel the benefit.

And just to be clear, if you are consciously having a lie in on a day off because that will make you feel your best, go for it.

Avoiding Distraction

I asked a client to estimate how much time they gave to unnecessary distraction in a day, and the answer shocked us both. She spent a week or so consciously considering that through her everyday experiences, and the answer was more than two hours daily! What do you think your answer would be to this question?

Technology clearly plays a big part, with notifications coming through multiple channels, the expectation for instant responses to messages, and calls that we feel duty bound to answer. I don't think we can overestimate how much this disrupts our flow, and affects our efficiency. We essentially allow someone else to spend our time without choice, permission or intention.

Technology isn't the only source of distraction though – it could be related to people, tasks, what's on TV or something happening outside. It could even be your own avoidance technique – clearing out a cupboard instead of writing an important report due tomorrow (sound familiar?).

Some distractions are good – they nourish us, we engage deliberately and we know when we need to draw it to a close to avoid it adding to our stress. Most distractions don't fall into this category, because they are .... distractions.

I'd encourage you to consider which distractions are stealing your time and contributing to stress along with those that feel good to you, and help build your resilience.

Does Your Time Need Your Attention?

If you are someone who consistently doesn't have enough hours in the day, feels overstretched and overwhelmed, and never gets a minute for yourself, then it will be worthwhile considering how to be a master of your own time.

12

HOW TO MOVE FORWARD

I've shared a lot of options and detail throughout this section, all with the intention of giving you a broad menu of choices that can help you have it all, without burning out. Let's bring it all together in a short summary so you can easily focus on what steps to take next.

Know What You Want

If there's only one message you take away from reading this book, this is it. If you want to have it all, then you first need to have a clear understanding of what your 'all' is. Chasing someone else's dream or society's version of success without checking if it's what you really want will only lead you to disappointment and stress. Knowing what you want and why is a critical starting point. Without it you'll end up chasing your tail, experiencing inner conflict, and never being as satisfied as you could otherwise be.

If you know what brings you joy and what's most important to you, and consciously pursue a life that achieves those things, I believe that will lead to more fulfilment, health and happiness. It doesn't mean you need every step figured out; it's more about knowing that you're heading in the right direction. Using a combination of thinking and feeling as your compass is a skill worth mastering.

In reality, you only need to know what's important to you for the foreseeable future. Whilst some will urge you to have your long term plan established up front, I believe that our experiences along the way teach and guide us towards the next steps. Trying to figure out what you want in 20+ years' time can often lead to procrastination and inaction or making a guess so wild that it immediately sets you on the wrong path.

Putting in the work to achieve clarity on what you want is always a great investment. The more clarity you gain, the easier and quicker your decisions will be, the less distraction you will experience along the way, and the more fun you'll have on the journey. I really encourage you to take stock and work through this.

Set Yourself Up For Success

I've spent several chapters sharing resilience boosting options for a very important reason. Modern life is stressful and complicated, and if you approach it without the focus or tools for looking after yourself in the process, you will likely feel the consequences. Just like any important project, you must set yourself up for success with the right resources, information, checks and balances.

One of those critical resources is your ability to proactively build resilience and be able to more easily manage stress. Let me remind you of the areas that have been covered.

Be sure that you have things in your daily routine that nourish you and help you thrive. Not only will it be a boost to your health and wellbeing, but it will increase your capacity for handling stress well, and improve your enjoyment and fulfilment.

BREATHE
SLEEP
REST
HYDRATION
NUTRITION
MOVEMENT
ADDRESS ILL-HEALTH

CLEAR PURPOSE
TECHNOLOGY SWITCH OFF
MINDFULNESS
MEDITATION
GRATITUDE & APPRECIATION
MAKE YOUR PEACE
JOURNALING

REAL CONNECTION
MOOD HOOVERS & ENERGY VAMPIRES
KINDNESS
HUG IT OUT
LAUGHTER
CONNECTING THROUGH TECHNOLOGY

GREEN SPACE
LIGHT
NOISE
CLUTTER
KEEP IT CLEAN

SELF FIRST
SAYING NO
TIME TO GET UP
AVOIDING DISTRACTION

Take Consistent Action

Clearly there's some work to do to achieve clarity of direction and determine how you will set yourself up for success, but in order to move forward you have to be taking action in a consistent manner. The best laid plans are useless without action. It's important to find the right balance between planning and doing. You don't want to over-think and end up doing nothing, but neither do you want to dive straight in without direction.

Often it's not the getting started that's difficult; it's keeping going once you're off the blocks. Forming new habits is a hard thing to do and that's why it is really important to be driven by what's important to you and what brings you joy, and support yourself with things that truly nourish you.

You are hard-wired to stay the same and avoid change. Making change involves risk and danger and therefore the stress response kicks in and tells you "no, that's not going to happen". Can you remember times when you have justified your lack of action to yourself? For example, you have every intention of going for a run as soon as your alarm goes off. But what happens? Your alarm goes off, you remember your commitment, but then you decide to have a look at your phone first which takes fifteen minutes, and then you hear the wind outside, followed by you remembering that your trainers are in the car and you'll have to go outside first. No, now is not the time for that run, it's too risky.

We've all been there and I'm sure you can think of many examples where you talk yourself out of perfectly sensible and well intentioned plans. The good news is that you are hard-wired to do that. Your brain wants you safe and doing something different is the opposite of that. The bad news is that you have to deliberately and intentionally overcome that hard-wiring, and that isn't always easy.

This is where immediate and consistent action comes into force. To retrain your brain that your new resilience-boosting activity is safe and enjoyable you must take immediate action. Otherwise the doubt, distraction and inaction immediately take over. You have seconds for this, and nowhere near a minute, before you're talking yourself out of this new amazing thing you were going to do.

Once you have started taking action, you do that consistently for a period of time, typically a minimum of 3-4 weeks. Over time you'll meet less and less resistance, until you have that new habit well and truly formed. I'm not saying you'll always find it easy, but it is entirely possible.

Stay Focused, Yet Flexible

You've achieved clarity of direction, you've set yourself up for success and you're taking consistent action – excellent. A few different things can throw us off course, for example:

- The direction in which you're heading no longer feels right. The experiences, lessons and growth you've had along the way are telling you something's not quite right.
- An unexpected event or opportunity occurs and automatically changes your perspective or desired direction.
- You're feeling exhausted or unwell and, as such, are losing enthusiasm and motivation for taking consistent action.

The thing to know is that it's OK to adjust and change course. People do it all the time. The key is to ensure that you're changing course for the right reason and this in itself can be a tricky assessment.

- It could be that it's still the right path but your brain and stress response are putting up some resistance – if this is the case then an increased focus on what's most important to you and why, along with a prioritisation of resilience boosting activities can help.
- Or it could be the case that there's some adjustment needed – a marginal shift in direction – some tweaks that you can make easily.
- If, however, you are feeling that you need to completely change course then it's time to head back to the point of determining what brings you joy, what you really want and why. And you can

now do this with some additional and powerful insights.

Keep reminding yourself of the clarity and support you've put in place for yourself and stay focused on that, but similarly don't be afraid to change if you believe that's the right thing to do.

Celebrate Your Successes

It's an area that often gets overlooked, either because there's a rush to get to the next item on the list, or there's a dislike for the attention that can be associated with an achievement. Not only is there a feel-good factor associated with achieving a goal, but it's a great reinforcement to your brain that the change you have made is leading to a new safe place – something to be protected and cherished.

You don't have to host a party, but you do need to explicitly acknowledge progress and achievement to enable the reinforcement of your new habits. This could be telling a friend, writing it in your journal, shouting it from the rooftops or placing an advertisement on the side of a bus – whatever works for you!

Time for Your First Step

Before you continue I would strongly urge you to either take your next step right now or make an explicit commitment to something that you are going to do today or tomorrow. No matter how much you want to change and move forward, only positive action will get you there. This could be as simple as:

- I'm going to do 60 seconds of deep breathing right now.
- I'm going to explore what brings me joy for 30 minutes tomorrow, it's scheduled in the calendar and I know what I'm going to write on.
- I'm calling someone now to tell them that I won't be able to go to their event next month because I'm over-stretched.

Make a commitment, no matter how small, and take action before you turn the page. These little steps all contribute to moving us in the direction we want to go.

IMPROVING YOUR CHANCES

13

LET'S CHECK IN

Amidst the theory, stories, insight and advice, I've been asking you to tune in to how you think and feel, to review what's working for you and what isn't, to really appreciate and understand the direction that will bring you joy, and to start making those small steps. For some this is an interesting and exciting part of the journey; for others it may have become a little overwhelming. If it's the latter, remember it's only ever one small step at a time. There is no right or wrong way, just your way.

What you will have realised as you've been reading this book is that none of this is rocket science, yet because it involves personal action and change it becomes challenging to implement, particularly when you are experiencing high levels of stress. That's why people turn to others for support – their friends or family or a professional in the field. Do not allow yourself to consider that you have failed because you haven't mastered this yet. It is difficult and that's why it can be a struggle. And here's a secret – no-one ever truly masters the tricky balancing act of life because things are always shifting – but clarity, focus and intentional action to nourish ourselves make it a lot easier!

A Quick Review

Let's check in to understand how you are feeling and what's going on for you right now. That way, you can prioritise where you can best apply your focus. Here are a few simple questions for you to respond to:

- How would you assess your current level of stress on a scale of 1-10, 1 being very low and 10 being extremely stressed?
- How does this compare with your stress level a week ago?
- Do you have a good understanding of what your stressors are?
- Do you know how stress is physically and emotionally showing up in you?
- Do you feel able to bounce back quickly from a difficult or stressful time?
- Do you have a good understanding of what brings you joy?
- Do you know what is most important to you? Your 'why'?

- Do you have nourishing habits to build your resilience and boost your wellbeing?
- Do you know which nourishing habits work best for you?
- Are you consistently taking action to move forward?
- Have you acknowledged your successes so far?

Remember, there is no right or wrong, good or bad. It's just your reality check for today. Your 'yes' responses are something to acknowledge, celebrate and build on. Your 'no' responses are those which would benefit from some additional focus. If you have several 'no' responses, choose the one that feels the most important to work on first, and avoid attempting all of them at once.

It can be useful to come back to this checklist on a weekly basis. Given the pace of life it can be easy to miss your achievements, and this will help draw your attention to them.

What Can The Future Hold?

In previous chapters I've encouraged you to achieve a level of clarity regarding your moments of joy and how those can contribute to greater overall happiness, along with knowing what's really important to you in life – your why – your reason for doing things.

I am reminding you again, because with this clarity comes a greater ability to have it all, without burning out in the process. Achieving this clarity often involves the discovery that having it all is not the same as having everything; rather it's about experiencing all that is truly important to you, and which brings you joy in the process.

Let's consider that you do have it all, right now.

- How do you feel?
- What does it look like?
- Who is with you?
- What does a typical day involve?
- How are you spending your time?
- What is making you smile?
- What do you have around you?
- What is helping you feel your best?

I wonder how much of this is already present in your life and whether you've been able to acknowledge and celebrate that. Something for you to reflect on.

What's Getting In The Way?

We're usually highly skilled at answering this question! What are all the things, people, events, factors and situations that get in the way of us having it all?

It can be really helpful to get a piece of paper and write all of these down, uncensored and without any judgement.

What's stopping you experiencing joy? What's preventing you achieving what's really important to you? It isn't a trick question. Whatever you write on that piece of paper is your reality. Yes, you might be able to challenge yourself on some of them, but if you believe they are an obstacle write it down and acknowledge it.

Not having enough time usually features at the top of the list or is a contributing factor to other items, such as having too much on at work, over-committing to events and social occasions, and the children's social and activity schedule. Also featuring highly is not having the right amount of support, which could be related to your spouse, your family, your boss, your colleagues or your friends, for example.

At the beginning, all I suggest you do with your list is consciously increase your awareness of the items on there and then test the validity of it through your everyday experiences. Sometimes it's all that is needed to start influencing change. Bigger items may require some focus and work, but that will come in time.

What Will Help You Move Forward?

My sincere hope is that the contents of this book and your commitment to reading it will have provided useful information and sufficient motivation to take the next step and build the momentum you desire.

Nevertheless, change can be difficult to make, and so I want to share some tips for improving your chances of success. At the heart of these tips are three key factors:

- Accountability – being accountable to ourselves and to others is a great motivator and enables us to maintain focus, action and momentum.
- Guidance and Support – using the right information, expert knowledge and appropriate support structure is key to helping you explore new avenues, make decisions and work through any challenges.
- Intuition – critically, you must create the confidence to rely on your intuition. Whilst you might receive great information and advice from others, making your own choices is key.

You can go about doing this in a number of ways:

- Self-directed – if you want to drive this forward by yourself I would encourage you to write things down, make explicit commitments, schedule times for reviewing your progress, and keep your desired milestones visible. This approach requires determination, willpower, tenacity and resilience to be successful.
- Partnership – many people embark on a journey of change with someone who wants a similar outcome to them. You make commitments to each other,

often do activities together, check in with each other, offer support and help celebrate successes. These are really powerful partnerships when your goals, dedication and commitment are aligned. The key risk is one partner losing momentum which instantly impacts the other.

- Accountability Buddy – you can ask someone close to you to help keep you accountable to your commitments. They aren't on the same journey as you, but they have a vested interest to support you achieve what you want. Being clear on what support you want, your goals and objectives, and having regular reviews are all factors that can contribute to a successful approach.

- Expert Coaching Professional – working with the right coach will provide you with expert knowledge, professional guidance, objectivity, and consistent personalised support to enable you to achieve your goal. In order to get the best results through this route it's best if you can be fully open and honest, receptive to suggestion and challenge, and willing to commit to the relationship. If you choose the right coach they will naturally adapt to your needs.

When striving for improvement and transformation in ourselves it is normal to work through these approaches in order. If you are in a position to achieve the outcomes you desire by yourself, why wouldn't you? Similarly, if you have people in your life that you know are the perfect people to help you, then have the conversation as soon as possible. If you already know that you'll achieve the best results in the quickest time by taking on a coach, then start your research and determine who is the right fit for you.

There are always multiple ways to approach any challenge – use your intuition to choose the right one for you.

14

ACCELERATING YOUR PROGRESS

I f you want to accelerate your ability to make sustainable changes that will enable you be your best and thrive in all areas of your life, then having a coach is my recommendation. Whilst there are no overnight fixes when it comes to personal change, having the right coach by your side on the journey can undoubtedly improve your odds of getting on the right path to the right place within the right time frame.

I often come across both confusion and scepticism around the subject of coaching, from not really understanding what coaching is and what they could expect, right through to fearing a charlatan is going to take a good amount of their money in return for not very much. I understand this and that's why I want to share my knowledge of coaching, how to choose one, and hopefully answer any questions you may have about me.

What Is Coaching?

Put simply, I explain coaching as a partnership that helps unlock someone's potential in order for them to be their best in a particular area of life. It's a collaborative relationship requiring effort and focus from both parties, and with the common goal of enabling you to improve. It will always involve good conversation with lots of questions, suggestions and reflections. It usually involves some education and a little teaching to help you move forward, and maybe some sharing of stories and experiences where appropriate. There will be reviews, agreements and accountability. There should not be any judgement, telling or direct instruction as to what you 'must' do.

There is a fine balance between informing, encouraging and making suggestions as opposed to telling, instructing and directing. In my view coaching is about the former, and shouldn't really stray into the latter unless there is explicit agreement that such an approach is needed at the time.

You will come across coaching in many different fields, and it might not even be labelled as coaching. For example:

- Professional athletes may have a performance coach, a nutrition coach and a mindset coach – each relationship designed to help them perform at their optimum.
- Many business executives will have a coach to help them optimise their performance and will have

likely benefited from coaching throughout their career.

- Mental Health Professionals and Therapists will use coaching skills as part of their discipline enabling you to talk openly, reflect and explore.
- A Nutritional Therapist will be advising you on what steps to take whilst also coaching you to make the changes needed and adopt new habits for the future.
- A Personal Trainer will combine instruction as to what activities you should do and how, alongside encouraging you to adopt new exercise regimes through coaching in your session.
- A Teacher will clearly be teaching and instructing, but they are likely also coaching you to think in new ways, push your boundaries and explore different fields.

In essence there will be a coach for any subject where people want to improve or make change, whether that be related to work performance, career direction, relationships, health, personal style, sports, and so much more.

You will likely be coaching on a daily basis yourself, consciously or otherwise. For example, there will be times that you need to tell your child what to do, but there will be others where you are encouraging curious thought and exploration so they can discover some things for themselves. You will have experienced something similar at work. And I'm sure many of you have helped a friend find their own answer to a difficult question.

Clearly when you are working with a professional coach, they should always be in coaching mode. If it's with a friend or family member it's very easy for them to switch between questions, offering opinions, and telling you what they think you should do.

Coaching vs Mentoring

These terms are often used interchangeably and I do believe there's a high degree of overlap between them. Ultimately they are both focused on helping someone improve, advance and achieve their desired goals.

A mentor, in the traditional sense, is someone who's been there before you and is sharing their wisdom and guidance to help you follow in their footsteps. It assumes that their achievements are your aspirations and you have a desire to learn their approach and methods, whilst being able to avoid any mistakes they made along the way.

Coaching doesn't have the same prerequisite; the coach doesn't need to have already achieved what you aspire to. Their approach is to use their skills and techniques for enabling you to find the answers to any challenge or goal. They are focused on helping you to find your own way rather than learn directly from their experiences.

In reality, there will be a bit of both included. In my work, there is definitely a combination of coaching and mentoring depending on the needs of my clients and how I can best serve them.

I'd suggest not getting too hung up on whether someone calls themselves a mentor or a coach; the most important thing is that they are a good fit for you.

Individual vs Group Coaching

There are many group coaching programmes available these days so it's worth understanding the merits of each.

With individual 1-2-1 coaching the entire focus is on you, your needs and your progress. As a result the service is highly personalised and adaptable to suit you. It will carry a higher price tag reflecting the time and focus dedicated to you as an individual.

Group coaching is designed for like-minded individuals who are happy to be collectively guided by the coach through a mixture of learning approaches. You are usually being guided through the coach's blueprint for success, and for that reason you could consider it more like mentoring. Programmes typically include online modules, group calls for questions and sometimes a short period of individual coaching in front of your peers, an interactive peer community, resources and worksheets. Some more exclusive programmes will include dedicated 1-2-1 sessions too. They will carry a lower price tag than opting for 1-2-1 coaching with the same person.

Your goals, needs, style and circumstances will determine which is right for you.

Choosing A Coach

Once you've decided that coaching is right for you, finding the right coach can be a daunting prospect. Here are my suggestions in looking for the right person.

First, narrow your search:

- Know the general area you would like support with to enable you to be more specific. Performance at work, career choices, health or home, for example. It's OK if there is more than one area – that's helpful to know in itself.
- Reflect on whether you feel you need a mentor or a coach, or a combination of both. Do you want to follow in someone's footsteps or help in creating your own path?
- Consider any styles that have or haven't worked for you in the past, and whether that can help guide your choice.
- Work out what's really important to you in a coach, including the way they work. For example, is it important you see someone face to face, or does

your lifestyle mean a remote session would be better?

Next, start the search:

- Ask around. Coaching is a personal service so ask those people who may have used a coach for similar reasons. A personal referral is a great insight and you have the opportunity to ask lots of questions about their experience.
- Make your online search as specific as possible. Rather than 'coaching services in my area' you might be looking for 'coaching for resilience in north-west England' or 'overcoming fatigue and overwhelm', for example.
- Any coach should offer you the opportunity to speak to them before committing to anything. Make contact and ask to speak to them. If they are a good coach, they should be able to ask all the right questions to check if they can help you, but it is good to have a sense of what you want to find out before you start the call.
- Be certain that you feel comfortable speaking openly to them. Coaching is personal and to get the most from it you'll need to have confidence that you can open up quickly and easily.

Making your decision:

- Intuition will play a big part here, along with more practical factors like how they work and what it costs.
- Once you're comfortable with your choice get started as soon as possible – remember to take action that commits you quickly or you can easily start talking yourself out of it.
- If you're not going ahead with someone, let them know and don't shy away from telling them why. Most coaches are self-employed and would benefit hugely from this feedback.
- Celebrate this step – it's a big one!

What To Expect When Being Coached

If you've done your search thoroughly and your chosen coach has been forthcoming in their approach, then you will hopefully have a good sense of how things will run during the course of your programme. There will still be some unknowns such as how you'll feel during the process, how much you'll be able to share of yourself, the insights you will uncover and the direction you will take. This is completely normal and my recommendation is to trust yourself and your coach and go with it.

Your coaching programme is about more than the sessions themselves; it's about the work and reflection you do throughout the course of your programme and beyond. It's important to know that there's work for you to do if you want to get the most from it. You should expect to be challenged, face some thought-provoking questions and potentially be pushed beyond your comfort zone. You should also expect to be supported and encouraged. But more than anything, you should feel like you're in a partnership that has your best interests at the centre of it all.

My Experience With Coaching

I consider myself very fortunate having worked with multiple coaches throughout my career, the majority of which were funded and supported by the business I worked for. I've always had positive experiences and each relationship has helped me adjust and move forward, although a couple in particular I would consider life-changing. I don't use that phrase lightly; I genuinely mean that working with a coach at certain points has resulted in my life significantly changing course for the better.

I have always embraced the coaching process and thrown myself in to it wholeheartedly; I consider it a powerful part of my journey. I'm now self-employed and still make the investment in a coach, choosing the person right for me at the time. I view it as a core part of my business model and can't yet see a time when I'd be without one.

Coaching With Me

I am proud to now use the title of coach for my profession although the reality is I have enjoyed coaching and mentoring in business with success for many years. I've been on countless leadership development and training programmes, each with a significant focus on coaching, and I've seriously pursued my own continuous development in this area. I spent three years becoming qualified as a Nutritional Therapist, knowing with certainty of the link between our health, performance and fulfilment. I have no doubt that there will be more professional development in the coming years; my drive to personally develop and also improve what I can offer my clients is so strong.

But more than anything, my main driver for formally entering the world of coaching is because I connect with people, I genuinely care about their success, and I have a natural ability to get people talking, exploring and developing. My fulfilment from helping others move forward, overcome challenges and be able to thrive in work and life is off the charts. I love it!

In a subsequent chapter some of my clients will tell you what it's been like to work with me, but for now let me tell you about the work I do and how I help people.

On the face of it, the clients I work with vary significantly. Women and men, from their early 20s through to retirement age, from many different professions, family circumstances, socio-economic status and locations. However, as soon as you get to know these people you quickly understand the common themes:

- They are high achievers, very capable and with many future ambitions.
- They are go-getters, tenaciously 'pushing through' to get where they need to be.
- They are used to high pressure and the stress that goes with it; they may even crave this.
- They have had a stark realisation – that the stress they once craved has turned into overwhelm; that they no longer feel as well and energised as they used to; that they are losing their zest for life; or that in order to get to where they want to be they need improved clarity and strategies to keep themselves focused and thriving.
- Many are experiencing burnout to some degree.

Clients often say it can take some time for them to reach the point where they realise they will benefit from some support, their natural inclination being to resolve any problems themselves. The scarcity of time and reducing energy levels become obstacles to that being successful, after which they start to consider what could help them.

Once someone has reached out, the first step is always a conversation to explore what has led them to take that step, get to know each other a little and determine if we are a good fit for working together. I refer to this as a Discovery Call and make it easy by having a booking system on my website for it. It's free and without obligation – it is as important to me as it is to you that I feel confident in supporting you in your objectives.

When I first started out I used to offer single pay-as-you-go sessions, but quickly realised this didn't deliver the results either party desired. I now only work on a programme basis with a minimum number of sessions and time period, and unsurprisingly, client results are significantly improved. When someone agrees to a programme it means they are as committed as I am, and that mindset from the outset makes an enormous difference.

My method is simple and straightforward – I focus on having strong connection, deep conversation and a collaborative approach to the direction we take. There are no false promises of quick fixes or overnight transformations, but there is a guarantee of partnership, support, encouragement and challenge. This approach allows me to personalise and flex in order to best meet my client's needs. My intuition, experience and client feedback tells me this is the way to get the best results for the people I'm working with.

Amidst my coaching services, I'm able to offer a depth of experience from leadership, working in large corporates, my health and nutrition training, and of course my personal experience of experiencing chronic stress and burnout. I believe the combination is powerful and it clearly influences the clients I attract and the way I approach my work.

Many of my clients are living very busy lives and are in a different location to me, so we make use of the technology easily available today and connect through video conference. It's all about making the service and support easy to access and over 90% of my clients use this option.

One of the things I enjoy most about my work today is the enduring connection I have with many of my clients, social media making that much easier to achieve. There's nothing I enjoy more than clients getting in touch and letting me know what's going on for them and updating me on the latest. Coaching is not a transactional service; it's based on a professional connection that can have real meaning for both parties.

Nutritional Therapy & Health Coaching

I include nutrition and lifestyle guidance within my coaching programmes when it is relevant to the individual and their objectives. But when there is something more complex going on from a health perspective that requires specialist support then I wear my Registered Nutritional Therapist hat.

Nutritional therapy is often misunderstood with people thinking that the discipline is all about weight management and diets for losing weight. The discipline is far more sophisticated than that and uses nutritional and lifestyle science to understand the root cause of health issues and promote optimal health. It is recognised as a complementary medicine and can be used to support those with chronic health conditions as well as those who are proactively looking to improve their wellbeing.

Again, I only work on a programme basis when providing this service and am careful which cases I take on, ensuring that I can help. As with any health discipline, practitioners tend to have their specialisms and mine is in the space of stress and stress-related conditions. That in itself is quite broad, with stress having an impact on many areas of our health such as digestion, immunity and hormone balance, for example.

A fascinating area of nutritional therapy is the ability to recommend and interpret certain clinical tests as part of the investigative approach to understanding the root cause of any ill-health. It can provide such beneficial insights allowing you to really target a protocol. The most common tests I run in my practice are related to stress levels, digestive health, thyroid function, nutrient status and female hormone balance.

Of course I bring a strong element of coaching to my work. Whilst nutritional therapy involves guidance and instruction, I find that coaching people through the changes required is enormously beneficial.

My Services

You can look on my website for details of the services available, but in a nutshell they include:

- The Resilience Formula online programme – if you've enjoyed the content of this book, then this online programme takes it further and deeper.
- Personal Coaching – where you and I work together one-on-one to enable you to achieve your goals, get thriving, and delivering your best at work.
- Nutritional Therapy and Health Coaching – my specialist service for more complex health conditions.
- Health Testing – working with reputable UK laboratories I can offer numerous health testing options, usually as part of a coaching or nutritional therapy programme.

I also have a free Facebook community and have written this book with the intention of providing people with easy access to this type of information, along with the opportunity to explore what support is right for them.

The Discovery Call is always a critical part of the process, helping me to recommend the right service for you, and sometimes tweaking what's on offer to suit your needs better. Don't be afraid of having a conversation – I know the first step can be the hardest and I will always make the call as easy as possible for you.

Where You Can Find Me

If you want to get in touch there are several ways you can connect, all of which have links on my website. You can find me in these places:

- www.deborahbulcock.com – my website through which you can find my contact details, the links to my social media, and book a Discovery Call.
- On Facebook – my community has the same name as this book, 'Have It All Without Burning Out', and my business page is 'Deborah Bulcock – Coaching and Consulting'.
- On LinkedIn you will find me under my name, and I'm still the only person with that name and spelling!
- Whilst not as active on Instagram and Twitter my handle on both is @deborahbulcock.

I look forward to connecting with you.

What About Organisations?

Yes I do also work with organisations …. on to the next chapter.

15

SUPPORTING YOUR TEAM

I f you lead a team of people, are in a role that supports people in other departments, or are running your own business then you will have acute awareness of how individual and team performance influences organisational performance. You will know that health, wellbeing and engagement are integral to that performance and I'm sure you will have observed how stress can also have a negative influence.

Shocking Insights

Here are some statistics that still astound me, despite having read the reports several times:

- According to the Health & Safety Executive Stress Report 2018, 15.4 million working days were lost due to work-related stress, depression or anxiety in

Great Britain across a twelve month period in 2017/2018. The impact of this lost time was reported to have costs employers a total of £26 billion or an equivalent of £1,035 per employee, per year.

- A review of recent studies by Deloitte in 2017 suggested that the loss of productivity from mental health related presenteeism, when employees operate at less than full capacity due to ill-health, costs the UK economy £15.1 billion per annum.
- A report published by the Financial Times and Vitality in 2019 showed that 34% of UK employees indicated they have felt unwell because of work-related stress and that this was more common amongst employees who earn lower incomes.

There are many more such statistics, and the information I've read from the US is often more striking. The bottom line is that stress is having an impact on individuals and therefore on teams and organisations. My objective is to help teams turn this on its head – when individuals are thriving in all aspects of their lives, then the organisation they work for will clearly benefit. With that objective in mind, I work with teams in a handful of different ways.

Helping Teams

Having spent over twenty years leading teams in large corporates I have to say the opportunity to support teams within organisations brings me great delight. I love becoming part of that team for the period I'm working with them, helping them to achieve their goals and do so in a way that leaves them energised rather than clinging on by their fingernails.

We must get past the point where culture drives someone to work so hard that they sacrifice their personal life and health to the extent that they reach burnout. No-one wins in that situation. Yet everyone wins when people are thriving. Surely it's a no-brainer.

There are a number of ways in which I help teams and organisations and they can largely be categorised as:

- 1-2-1 Coaching – in the last chapter I told you about my coaching approach. The main difference here is that the organisation is sponsoring, funding and benefitting too.
- Group Coaching –involving small teams of people interested in exploring similar subjects coming together in facilitated sessions for coaching as a group.
- Workshops and Presentations – I run bespoke sessions on most topics under the broad heading of personal effectiveness and wellbeing, but the majority of the sessions I run are focused on the subjects of stress, resilience and the link to performance and wellbeing. All sessions can be run in person or virtually.

- The Resilience Formula – this online course can be run as a supported programme where I take a team of people through the programme over a number of weeks. It's a cost effective and powerful way to take people on a self-development journey to increased resilience. And the side-effect is a more connected team.
- Consultancy – when leaders need some hands-on support I'm there in a consultancy capacity, on just about anything where people and performance are concerned.
- Partnering – often people ask me for a combination of 'all the above' over a period of time, and that's when we step into a partnership. I'm by your side, responding and adapting the approach to suit your needs.

Often I work with a team on more than one of these areas over a period of time. We may start with a workshop which identifies the need for some individual coaching, for example. The key for me is that it doesn't all have to be worked out before we start; it's just important to get started.

Resilience for Leaders – A Few Kind Words

This signature workshop is all about understanding the subject of stress and how it can affect us in life and at work, followed by exploring how to proactively manage stress and build resilience, before working through team and individual actions for positive change. The team discussion is always powerful and probably the most important element of the session. Here's some abbreviated extracts from what attendees have said.

> *"Deborah delivers on a 'fluffy' topic in a way that feels weighty and relevant. The science and biology is so interesting and helps me appreciate how to use it to my advantage."*

> *"We are already having different conversations as a team and it's improving our relationships and delivery."*

> *"Burn-out is an emotional topic for me ... I thought you brought this to life superbly, offering guidance on how to prevent it happening to me or anyone else close to me."*

> *"Really beneficial. I have had struggles with stress and anxiety for many years. It's been great to understand stress on a more scientific level and tactics to combat it."*

Working In Partnership

I know what it's like to be busy running a team and receiving support from a third party. I realise there is an investment of time on your behalf to set things up in addition to the ongoing requirement to monitor and review. That's why when I'm working with a team I operate very much as your business partner, vested in your goals and objectives, and making the oversight of my contribution easy and efficient for you.

You can expect me to respond to your needs and circumstances, but also provide the healthy challenge and guidance you would expect from a business partner. There is no 'one size fits all' approach and whilst we will optimise any synergies available we will also tailor to suit you and your team. When we find that sweet spot of a strong partnership you should be getting to where you want faster and with less effort and stress than doing it alone.

Because partnership is important to me, I work with organisations where that is important to you too. It's how I believe we will enjoy mutual success and enjoy the journey together.

How To Get Started

Exploring how we can work together and setting things up in an organisational context can take time; I appreciate that and I've been in the same position. But you don't need to know exactly what you want before picking up the phone; it's much more effective to work through that together.

Whilst some engagements are signed and sealed within a week of the first meeting, they are few and far between. My assumption is that there will be several discussions and some back and forth in order to get to the right outcome for you and your team. Therefore the key is to start the discussion sooner rather than later.

You can schedule a call directly with me via my website or contact me directly, and that's how these engagements usually begin. I look forward to hearing from you.

16

I AM PLEASED TO INTRODUCE

I wanted to introduce you to five of my amazing clients that I have had the privilege of working with over the past year, in order to provide you with an insight into their lives, how they have found the experience of working with me and what is different for them as a result of the commitment and investment they have made in themselves.

I have asked each individual exactly the same questions and here's what they had to say.

Meet Lisa

Service Provided: Team Support – Workshop, Presentation, Coaching, Leadership Partnering.

Lisa is a Director in a large global organisation leading a team of professionals providing a critical service across multiple functions in the business. Foreseeing lots of business change and increasing pressure Lisa wanted to be proactive in offering some support to her team. I have worked in partnership with Lisa to provide the full-day Resilience for Leaders Workshop to her leadership team, a presentation to her broader team, and individual and group coaching programmes for many of her team too. Her proactivity has undoubtedly paid dividends and our partnership continues. Here's how Lisa described her experience.

Tell us a bit about yourself

I'm a single mum of a 16 year old lively and independent teenager. We live in Manchester in the north of England with our dog, and together we enjoy days out, good food, walks in the countryside and plenty of holidays. I'm very close to my wider family and have a great circle of friends who I manage to socialise with frequently. It's important to me to have downtime with friends and family, in addition to some solo time. I'm an avid football fan and get to matches as often as possible.

I've been in corporate life for 26 years at the same company, have progressed through the ranks doing lots of different roles and now hold a large senior role carrying significant responsibility. I work from home in Manchester, but also spend a number of days every month at head office in London. I'm managing this balance of working at home and away successfully and I believe that's because I do it on my terms, always deliver, and make it work for me, my team and the business.

What was the situation that led you to look for support?

We had a new CEO with a new strategy and I knew there would be a heavy reliance on my team and me to support the changes that would be required. There would be no additional resource to deliver this, despite changing and increasing work pressures. I could have let the team get on with it; they are more than capable. However I wanted to give them everything they needed to perform and succeed – for themselves and for the business.

How did you find the experience of working with me?

Because of your background, both professionally and personally, it was easy for you to quickly assess and understand the situation and come up with options for supporting us. It's clear that you care deeply about people and this subject, and that you get as much out of seeing my team thrive as I do.

You have a passion, drive and energy that not only allows you to deliver, but that keeps me accountable for seeing things through. In a high pressure work environment it can be easy to let these things slip, but you have ensured it is has stayed firmly on our agenda and that has been of great benefit.

My team feel fortunate to be working with you, as do I.

What have been the main benefits?

- The workshop and presentation certainly had an

impact – people are still talking about it a few months on and it has provided a safe and common language for people to use in relation to stress.

- The team in general are thinking more about each other, overall team-working has improved, and I see people flocking to support each other when there is a request for assistance.
- I've been amazed at the speed at which people have improved and accelerated as a result of the individual coaching. I have seen confidence and self-belief increase significantly, and I know the benefits have been to their whole life, not just work.
- Overall the team are more engaged and happier at work, so much so that other teams are asking about it.
- On a personal level your support for the team has provided me with the capacity to step-up, to be more strategic, and to focus on leading the entire team more effectively.

Who would you recommend my services to, and why?

Any leader who:

- Wants their team to thrive in all areas of their lives.
- Really understands the benefit of people bringing their whole self to work, in that it helps them deliver great business outcomes.
- Wants to build their team, the support they can

offer each other, and the strength of their relationships.

- Understands that stress and mental health are not only integrally linked, but are very grey areas – there is no black and white, and people need to be treated as individuals.
- Appreciates that corporate life always becomes more challenging year on year – by focusing on your people you will always get a higher return to meet that challenge.

What words of wisdom can you offer to the readers of this book?

- Watching people grow and develop is a brilliant experience – do all you can to create that for your team.
- It is important to have faith in your people, especially when they haven't got faith in themselves.
- Trust your instincts and believe in the capability and determination of your team.

Meet Marina

Service Provided: Company Sponsored Coaching

Marina is a leader in a large corporate who is completely dedicated to delivering for the business, whilst also developing herself in the process. Following a particularly demanding and pressured period at work Marina felt her confidence, energy and overall zest decreasing rapidly. Following discussions with her line manager some coaching was recommended to help her recover from the tolls of extreme stress, get her energy and confidence back, and to achieve clarity on her future direction. I found Marina open, receptive and determined from the outset and the speed of progress she made continues to astound me. Here's what she has to say about her experience.

Tell us a bit about yourself

I'm 45 years old and a single mum, after divorcing four years ago. At the same time as my divorce I took the decision to move country for my career and took a new role with the same company based in London. My sons are 16 and 10 and we live together not far from where I work. Whilst teenage tantrums may be at their peak, we enjoy our family time together. I enjoy learning new things and pushing myself a little, both in work and life. I like to go for long walks whenever I can and I love to read, although the latter feels like a real luxury due to time constraints.

I'm a senior manager in a global institution and enjoy my work. My career is very important to me and I'm not afraid of the hard work that's required to achieve what I want for myself and my family.

What was the situation that led you to look for support?

I had spent nearly a year in an extremely demanding position where work pressures were very high. I was working 24-7, always on standby and never able to switch off. Despite working so hard nothing was ever good enough and I never felt appreciated or valued for what I was contributing. My confidence was at an all-time low and I felt beaten down. I had tried my hardest, yet felt like a failure. I've been brought up to be strong, keep going and not ask for help. But the time came when I had no choice but to speak to my line manager and seek support.

The pressures I was experiencing at work had many knock-on impacts. I wasn't spending enough time with my boys, when I was with them I was often distracted with work, and I was losing my patience much more than I should. With little time for myself I had stopped exercising, eating well and doing the things I enjoy to look after myself. I started living in fear of the ping of another email and I would feel this in the pit of my stomach. I wasn't sleeping well and would wake up thinking of work. I struggled to think clearly which just exacerbated the problem.

How did you find the experience of working with me?

In one phrase, I would say it has been life-changing. I have changed the way I think about things, in life and at work. I didn't know how to cope with the loud critical inner voice I was experiencing and you helped me so much with that. Everything we have covered has been practical; small things that are easy to try and implement. You always helped me focus on the positive and feel good about what I was doing.

What have been the main benefits?

Being able to think more clearly and differently. I am much more positive in my outlook and feel that I know what is important to me. I have learned new ways to help me manage stress that feel sustainable in my busy life. I now approach things looking at my whole life, not just one aspect. And importantly, I have a much improved balance between time with my family and my time at work.

Who would you recommend my services to, and why?

Anyone who is feeling very stressed, pulled down, or when things aren't working out as you had planned. You need to come to it with an open mind to get the most from it. Many of the tips Deborah shares aren't rocket science, but the encouragement she gives you means you are more likely to do them consistently and feel the benefits.

What words of wisdom can you offer to the readers of this book?

Don't take everything too seriously!

Meet David

Service Provided: Coaching

David is a consulting professional who takes great pride in his work and the relationships he develops with his clients.

He's very private and reaching out to someone he didn't know will have been a courageous step for him. David has a high level of self-awareness which had allowed him to identify some potential difficulties ahead and take the proactive steps to get some support in place. I think he surprised himself with his level of openness, the areas we explored and what he ultimately achieved from the work he did during our time working together. I was constantly impressed with David's depth of self-insight, willingness to try out new things and reflect on what was right for him. Undoubtedly, David took his self-development and personal growth as seriously as his professional work, and that brought him amazing outcomes.

Tell us a bit about yourself

I'm self-employed working as a consultant and have been doing that for eight years now. I work with one company at a time and can stay with them for anything from three months to well over a year. I really value the clients that I work with and take my work and my brand very seriously. In recent years I've taken on more senior positions that come with additional responsibility. It's important to me do a good and professional job for my clients, and as a result work probably takes a bigger proportion of time in my life than it might do for others.

I'm part of a big family and love spending time with my nieces and nephews, taking them out and spoiling them, before handing them back over. I then have the luxury of going on my merry way. My family aren't all local to me and I do experience a bit of guilt for not seeing them enough. I'm keen on health and fitness and believe in the benefits of a healthy body and mind. I like to explore new places and have just started doing more of that through my holiday travel.

What was the situation that led you to look for support?

I was coming to the end of an engagement with a client that I had really enjoyed working with. During my time with them I had set up a new team from grass-roots and there-fore had a real emotional connection with them. I knew that I would soon need to hand that team over and felt it was going to be difficult for me. I wanted to be proactive and decided to seek support.

In addition to this I felt that work had become everything and was occupying far too much of my life. I wasn't doing much outside of work and I was keen to make a change to that. This was making me unhappy and as a result I wasn't enjoying my work as much.

How did you find the experience of working with me?

I found the practical and pragmatic side of your approach really easy to engage with – your online booking system, being able to do our sessions on video conference, and you being very accessible to contact. You always sent me some short session notes afterwards and this was a great memory jog for me.

I was really surprised at how quickly we developed a strong connection. I can remember our first session vividly it was that impactful; I was comfortably sharing things I wouldn't even talk to my good friends about. I trusted you instantly and you provided a safe environment to talk and explore. I enjoyed your subtle way of making suggestions and exploring options – never with any expectation or judgement.

What was also helpful was that you had worked in similar environments and so you understood immediately what I was talking about. Your credibility as someone who had worked in the corporate environment and your subject matter expertise was really beneficial.

Whilst I came to you with very specific objectives in mind, as we went through our sessions more came up in a very organic way. You responded to this with ease and flexibility.

What have been the main benefits?

There have been many, but I think the main ones are:

- I'm now much more positive within myself.
- During our time working together I've managed a home move, a new role and a holiday – this had the potential to be really challenging, but instead I got through it all really well.
- It's taught me to test my understanding and assumptions with close friends and this improved

communication has allowed me to feel more relaxed.

Who would you recommend my services to, and why?

There's such a broad range of things that you can help with – it doesn't have to be industry or role specific and I think there is something for everyone. Anyone trying to better themselves or evaluate how they are doing things, and anyone feeling burnt out or wanting more resilience. The person does have to bring to the table an open mind – that's really important.

What words of wisdom can you offer to the readers of this book?

If you are taking up coaching with Deborah enjoy the process and make the most of the time. The sessions go quickly so ask all the questions you need to. It's a magical hour in the week and so have a great conversation and don't hold anything back.

Remember that you don't have to do things on your own. Others can help you professionally and personally and I would encourage you to engage in the support that is available.

Meet Katie

Service Provided: Coaching

Katie is a vibrant, caring and sociable woman, one of those who looks fabulous whenever you see her and always has a big smile and something lovely to say. She's always there for anyone who needs her and prides herself on that. She has a husband and two children who are at the centre of her world, closely followed by all her family and large circle of friends. Katie is undoubtedly always on the go and there's never a dull moment. She's strong, resilient and resourceful, never one to say no to a challenge or opportunity. When Katie got in touch the balance had been tipped and busy had turned into overwhelm. With an extremely hectic life to manage it wasn't an option to stop and take stock. Katie wanted someone by her side to guide her step-by-step back to vibrancy and daily enjoyment. Here's how Katie describes it.

Tell us a bit about yourself

I'm in my early 40s, married, with two young boys. I now work part-time in our family business, following previous full-time positions in a large corporate. My husband can also work away from home at times and so that adds another dimension to manage.

As a family we have an exceptionally busy lifestyle; I'd even call it chaotic at times. During the week we are balancing work, school, lots of activities, and social commitments. At the weekends we are always on the go and doing something, usually as a family and with our friends and their families. We enjoy having people over and we're often doing the same at other people's houses. As a result there's very little downtime for us and no two days are the same.

We take as many frequent breaks as we can so we will always have time for just the four of us.

What was the situation that led you to look for support?

I'm definitely over ambitious with the time that I have, always juggling too much, and finding it difficult to say no to things. The fear of missing out was strong and I felt really bad if I had to say no something or let someone down. I had started to get stressed out and emotional, with my moods varying and it got to a point where I wasn't able to easily prioritise day-to-day. I was on an emotional roller coaster and was becoming upset far too easily. I was definitely doing too much, over-committing and was run down and tired as a result. I had no get up and go anymore and was very sluggish. My nutrition and exercise was suffering and there was no time for me.

How did you find the experience of working with me?

A relief! I immediately felt like there was light at the end of the tunnel. I knew I needed to do something, but I didn't know what that was. It felt like a weight was lifted for you to take the reins and guide me through. There were so many simple things that I could do to make myself feel better – the things you don't even consider when you're really stressed out.

Your knowledge was amazing and very informative. You were always friendly and understanding and there was never any judgement. I didn't once feel vulnerable and you made it so easy to open up. Nothing was ever repetitive or boring; there was always something to learn and I like how you followed it up with notes and handouts.

What have been the main benefits?

Over and above anything else has been family time. This is always my priority and I feel I now have a better relationship with my children and we are spending more quality time together. I feel more relaxed about what I prioritise and what I have to say no to. There's much less guilt and anxiety associated with that now. I manage to have more me time and enjoy it. Everything seems to have fallen into place with how we look after ourselves. The pressure is off!

Who would you recommend my services to, and why?

Anyone who is feeling really stressed out and anxious. Those who are struggling to put themselves first and want to make a change. Also anyone who is really interested in the nutrition and health side of things. The lifestyle we lead and the stress we experience are all so inter-connected.

It's important to be committed to yourself when doing this. The guidance and support is there, but you have to do things whether that's practise something new or research, for example.

What words of wisdom can you offer to the readers of this book?

Don't put it off – do something now and make the first step. Health is so important and you have to put it to the top of the list, otherwise things will suffer in the long run. Only you can start the ball rolling.

Meet Martin

Service Provided: Coaching

Martin is a fun-loving and sociable man in his early 30s determined to enjoy life fully, whilst also seeing through his ambitions to achieve great things in his career. He takes his professional and personal development very seriously, striving to learn and grow at every opportunity. In recent years he has progressed his career at an accelerated rate and was feeling that this had the potential to negatively affect his health. Noticing a dip in energy and motivation, yet keen to keep progressing towards his goals, Martin took a proactive approach by getting in touch for support. As a result of taking action before things had deteriorated he was able to quickly return to a vibrant and positive place, enabling him to keep his performance strong at work without the need to sacrifice his personal life. The perfect outcome for him. Here's what Martin had to say about his experience.

Tell us a bit about yourself

I'm a project management professional working in a variety of roles on change programmes for large organisations. The environments I work in are high pressure and demanding, and whilst I tend to thrive on that, it can also sometimes take its toll. I do this work as an independent contractor and so this tends to involve quite a bit of travelling and working away. As a result my home life can feel quite fragmented at times.

My family and friends are extremely important to me and I love spending time with them whenever I can. I have a busy social life, and work hard to fit it all in. I like to stay in shape, be healthy and keep fit – these are areas that can easily get compromised when things get too busy.

What was the situation that led you to look for support?

I'm 31 years old and recognise that the career path I'm choosing for myself can have a negative impact on my balance of life. This has sometimes manifested as sleep disruption, my energy levels being low and fluctuating throughout the day, lots of worry and overthinking, having less patience, and generally not feeling as well as I could. I knew I had been endlessly chasing my career goals and wanted to find a way to thrive in work and life. As I was taking on more senior roles I became much more aware that something could give; that the balance was becoming too delicate. I was already starting to sacrifice my spare time, I just didn't have the energy to enjoy it. Something had to change.

I knew I had to look after my wellbeing in order to achieve everything I wanted to. I have a good level of self-awareness and already knew that I valued coaching and mentoring. I've always seen real benefit in self-examination, learning, accountability, progression – and doing it all in an accelerated way.

How did you find the experience of working with me?

It's been a really positive experience. It has been great to work with someone who has a shared professional background as that's made all the conversations really easy. It meant we could quickly get to the point without spending lots of time on explanation. I've enjoyed that I've been learning a lot and that it's been quite an intuitive and evolving process. I particularly like that you don't present yourself as the oracle – you are very real and it always feels like we are on the journey together.

What have been the main benefits?

There have been lots in many areas of my life:

- I've experienced notable improvements with my sleep and energy levels as a result of the changes I've made to my nutrition, lifestyle and mindset. My friends have even commented on the positive changes saying I'm chirpier and in a better mood,

that I'm sharper and more vibrant, that I look well
and even my skin has improved.

- My confidence has increased, I'm handling
  challenges better and don't seem to get flustered
  like I used to.
- I've taken a step up professionally whilst also
  making all of these improvements personally and I
  wouldn't have been able to do that alone in these
  timescales.
- Most importantly I've got a really good
  understanding of how to keep myself in a good
  place – I know which levers to pull if things start to
  feel difficult.
- I'm also applying what I'm learning to the
  workplace, considering how I can help my team to
  thrive.

Who would you recommend my services to, and why?

Someone who is willing to be open and honest, and at times
vulnerable – that's how you get the most from coaching
with Deborah. If you're feeling exhausted, are finding
things a struggle and your performance and enjoyment are
deteriorating then this could really help you. Even if you
can't put your finger on what's wrong. I'd also recommend
it to anyone who works in a professional capacity because
Deborah gets it – she's been there and really understands
the pressure and environment.

What words of wisdom can you offer to the readers of this book?

- When you are on your own journey don't beat yourself up about the pace of change – you are going at the right pace for you.
- It's OK to make small changes. The progress is still massive even if you don't realise it at the time. Have patience with yourself.
- Working with what you've got and making small improvements is the best way forward, especially when you are really busy.

My Reflections

As you can imagine it was quite emotional talking through these questions and answers with my clients and it served to reinforce my chosen path. Helping people overcome challenges and achieve these things is a real privilege and enormously rewarding. As a coach you are listening, understanding, questioning, encouraging, suggesting and supporting. As the person being coached you are the one doing all the heavy lifting. But as these stories suggest, the load is lighter with someone by your side.

17

FINAL WORDS

So now it's over to you.

I hope this book has provided you with the knowledge, insight and inspiration that I intended it to have.

I hope you can see more clearly your path to having it all without burning out, which in itself brings you joy and a sense of fulfilment.

Remember:

- Focus on your moments of joy and make the most of them.
- Having it all means pursuing what is important to you.
- Having it all doesn't mean doing and having everything.
- You already have the answers, although it is

common for those to be buried beneath confusion –
don't beat yourself up about that.

- Small steps will lead to great places.
- You don't have to travel alone.

I wish you joy and fulfilment as you thrive in all areas of your life.

With love and gratitude,

Deborah.

ABOUT THE AUTHOR
DEBORAH BULCOCK

COACH | CONSULTANT | NUTRITIONAL THERAPIST

As with most people, my career has been a journey of many twists and turns, although the common thread has always been supporting others to excel in achieving their goals.

I began my career in the financial services industry, where I was fast-tracked to director level. With two business degrees, boundless energy and bundles of ambition, success came quickly. I loved leading and developing large scale teams to perform and transform and made some of my closest friendships whilst doing so. But after 20+ years of performing at the height of my ability - without the right support structures or balance in my life - burnout was inevitable.

My recovery forced a long hard look at how I was living life at home and work, and piqued my interest in natural health both personally and professionally. Part-time business and part-time study for three years allowed me to add a new string to my bow as a Registered Nutritional Therapist.

For a few years I juggled two careers – corporate consulting alongside running my Health Coaching practice, but then the lines began to blur, the overlap became striking and it made sense to create a business that combined all of my experience. Now I support individuals to thrive amidst their busy lives, thereby enabling them to excel and succeed at work and in life.

My clients tell me that I help them cut through the noise, making complex subjects simple and accessible, and enabling them to take action and maintain momentum. Helping others to thrive in work and life is my passion and coaching is at the heart of everything I do.

Where You Can find Me

Website: www.deborahbulcock.com

Resource Centre: www.deborahbulcock.com/haveitall

Facebook group: https://www.facebook.com/
groups/HaveItAllWithoutBurningOut/

- linkedin.com/in/deborah-bulcock-coaching
- facebook.com/deborah.bulcock
- instagram.com/DeborahBulcock
- pinterest.com/deborahbulcock
- twitter.com/deborahbulcock

Lightning Source UK Ltd.
Milton Keynes UK
UKHW041845021120
372685UK00009B/647/J